Clouds of Secrecy

Clouds of Secrecy

The Army's Germ Warfare Tests over Populated Areas

LEONARD A. COLE

Foreword by Alan Cranston

ROWMAN & LITTLEFIELD
Publishers

ROWMAN & LITTLEFIELD PUBLISHERS, INC.

Published in the United States of America
by Rowman & Littlefield Publishers, Inc.
A Member of the Rowman & Littlefield Publishing Group
4720 Boston Way, Lanham, Maryland 20706
www.rowmanlittlefield.com

12 Hid's Copse Road
Cumnor Hill, Oxford OX2 9JJ, England

British Library Cataloguing in Publication Information Available

Library of Congress Cataloging-in-Publication Data

Cole, Leonard A., 1933–
    Clouds of Secrecy.
    Includes Index.
    1. Biological Warfare—Study and teaching—United States. 2. Biological Warfare
        Environmental aspects—United States. I. Title.
    UG447.8.C65   1987 358'.38   87–12777

    ISBN 0-8476-7579-3 (alk. paper)
    ISBN 0-8226-3001-X (pbk.: alk. paper)

Printed in the United States of America

♾™ The paper used in this publication meets the minimum requirements of American
National Standard for Information Sciences—Permanence of Paper for Printed Library
Materials, ANSI/NISO Z39.48-1992.

Contents

Appendices

Foreword

B IOLOGICAL WEAPONS are particularly heinous. Experts describe them as weapons to "distribute living organisms, usually bacteria or viruses, to disable or kill an enemy by causing disease."

The atrocities of chemical warfare during World War I led to one of the farthest reaching agreements of modern times, the Geneva Protocol of 1925. That treaty condemned chemical and biological weapons and prohibited their use. Efforts to ban these two types of weapons continue. The most recent agreement is the Convention on the Prohibition of the Development, Production, and Stockpiling of Bacteriological (Biological) and Toxin Weapons and on their Destruction, signed in 1972. The U.S. and the Soviet Union were among the signatories to both conventions.

The Reagan Administration, however, has accused the Soviet Union of violating the Biological Weapons Convention. The Administration claims the Soviets are maintaining germ warfare plants and have used toxins in Afghanistan. It also alleges that the Laotians and the Vietnamese used toxins under Soviet supervision in Laos and Kampuchea, respectively. Independent scientists have disputed the Administration's allegations, however.

Military leaders have not considered biological weapons particularly reliable. They are difficult to control once released in a battle situation. Arms control specialists say that it is difficult to gauge just how effective these weapons would be in a specific battlefield situation. In addition, the infections they cause could spread beyond the battlefield.

But, some knowledgeable people caution that with advances in biotechnology, the use of biological agents will become more attractive as weapons, not only for armies, but for terrorists as well. This concern, together with the Administration's allegations about the Soviets, has reopened the controversy over biological weapons.

The current U.S. biological warfare program was intended by Congress simply to study ways to counter biological warfare agents (i.e., as defensive research.) The Reagan Administration says that as a matter of policy it is not developing offensive biological weapons. But as Leonard Cole suggests, unless one is constantly on guard, research in defensive biological weaponry can easily spill over into offensive research.

Such a step could be a major blunder. We do not need offensive biological weapons for a strong national defense. Moreover, the risks to the American population in producing such weapons domestically could be monumental.

Safety must be a primary concern in any research conducted with biological agents. *Clouds of Secrecy* studies one aspect of U.S. Army research carried out in the 1950s and the 1960s. The experiments sought to determine the vulnerability of populated areas to biological attack. Some of the experiments involved the release of supposedly harmless organisms which had properties resembling those of certain biological agents. The Army claimed the organisms were innocuous. But Cole presents evidence that those organisms were known to be harmful. He suggests this is still an open question despite the fact that the court ruled in favor of the government in a suit for damages brought by a San Francisco resident in 1981.

Leonard Cole's study is a responsible work. It adds measurably to the literature currently available on this highly controversial subject. It raises some legitimate issues that should be explored further.

The first of such issues is the safety of the experiments. Was the population in these areas ever at risk? What about the organisms that were released? Were they completely safe? Equally important is the fact that large segments of the population were subjected to these experiments without their knowledge.

Congress has already taken steps to see that there is no recurrence of such secrecy. In 1977 Congress passed legislation requiring the Department of Defense to notify Congress before conducting any experiments with biological or chemical agents using human subjects. My information is that no secret tests have been conducted since the late 1960s.

Cole makes abundantly clear his opposition to the Army's open air testing and his criticism of the methodology used. And he buttresses his objections with evidence from primary sources about the excesses in the Army program. All in all, Cole makes a good case for the need for continued Congressional oversight.

Alan Cranston,
U.S. Senator

Preface

THE NOVEMBER 17, 1986 issue of *Time* magazine carried a curious story about the origin of AIDS. It cited foreign press reports that the disease "is the result of U.S. germ-warfare experiments gone wild." United States officials blamed the Soviets for spreading unfounded rumors, and AIDS experts thought the proposition farfetched. Yet, as the article indicated, some respected doctors would not rule out the possibility. Their skepticism addresses the frustration felt by many about understanding a disease that seems to have come from nowhere. It also reflects a simmering disquiet about the nature of the United States biological warfare program.

The army has engaged in biological warfare research since World War II, and its official position is that no one outside its laboratories has ever been at risk. Contrary evidence shows the claim to be hollow. Even if the AIDS/germ warfare allegation proves groundless, other army experiments have endangered large segments of the public.

This book is about these experiments, tests in which clouds of bacteria and chemicals have been sprayed over populated areas. It examines the nature of the tests, their rationale, and the effects on the exposed human populations.

My inquiries took me considerable distances, from a hamlet in northern Scotland where American scientists once helped perform biological weapons tests, to Fort Detrick, Maryland, headquarters of the United States biological warfare program. I spoke with dozens of government officials and scientists who have been involved with the testing program. I also met with citizens whose lives it has affected. Many live near forbidden areas that remain contaminated by bacteria from earlier tests. Some have sued the government, claiming that the army's tests caused illness and death to family members.

The factual story unfolded from interviews as well as documents and court proceedings. But the interviews revealed another dimension. They underscored how intense and partisan is the issue of biological warfare testing. Scientists and officials who are associated

ix

with the U.S. biological warfare program make no apologies for testing in populated areas. Their reference point is national security. They believe the Soviet Union is violating the 1972 Biological Weapons Convention that prohibits the development, production, or stockpiling of biological weaponry. The Soviet threat, accordingly, should be addressed with additional defensive research that includes open air vulnerability tests.

Many scholars and scientists believe that claims about Soviet violations are exaggerated or untrue. They challenge the validity of the evidence, and argue that expanding the United States program may itself lead to violations of the Convention. In any case, they consider open air tests involving unsuspecting citizens to be unwarranted and reprehensible.

The two sides' distrust of each other echoes through the remarks by members of each. After a genial interview, a scientist at Fort Detrick, who had long worked in the biological warfare program, said, "You know, I wouldn't have taken this time with you if I didn't think you were one of us."

The comment made me uneasy. He evidently had interpreted my eagerness to learn about the army's vulnerability testing program as an endorsement of the enterprise. I demurred from asking what he meant by "one of us," but emphasized my intention to write fairly. While agreeing with the need for national defense, I said that I could understand why people might be critical of the open air tests.

Some time later a community activist, who is convinced that the army is engaged in illegal biological weapons research, said to me, "I'm glad you're on our side." I felt no more comfortable about being grafted to this side than the other. My uncritical inquiries again apparently led a conversation partner to presume that I agreed with his position. Whatever anyone's suspicions about the army's current activities, claims about illegal actions are gratuitous without evidence. Of central interest to this book, however, is the army's position that open air testing is not illegal, and the fact that it is now taking place.

The interviews revealed a powerful sense of "us" versus "them." The atmosphere is fraternity-like, clubby. Members of either side are wary of outsiders. Probably nothing the army says or does about biological warfare research will allay the suspicions of its most dedicated critics. But others remain understandably skeptical because of misleading statements by army spokesmen in the past, and confusion about current policies. Several questions about the U.S. biological warfare program remain unanswered, including the extent of people's exposure to bacteria during tests. The army's interests, and the nation's, would be served by dispelling suspicions and addressing such issues fully and candidly.

Many people in and out of government shared their wisdom with me. Some are cited by name in the course of the narrative, many more are not, but I am grateful to all. Joan Aron, Ruth Cole, Norman Covert, Clifford Grobstein, Edward Nevin 3d, Jeremy Paxman, Robert Sinsheimer, Lawrence Ware, and Arthur Westing were especially helpful. They provided documents, background material, or insightful comments about the manuscript, and for their help I express my debt and appreciation.

PART ONE
OVERVIEW

1

Clouds of Secrecy: Introduction

DURING THE 1970s, Americans learned that for decades they had been serving as experimental animals for agencies of their government. The Central Intelligence Agency had secretly been dropping mind-altering drugs into the drinks of citizens to watch their reactions. The U.S. Public Health Service fooled syphilitic blacks into thinking they were undergoing treatment when in fact they were being observed as their disease worsened. In battlefield tests, soldiers were marched to nuclear explosion sites, where they were exposed to dangerous levels of radiation. For these experiments thousands of Americans served as unsuspecting guinea pigs, and many suffered illness and death as a consequence. But the scope of these projects was dwarfed by an army program to assess the country's vulnerability to biological weapons.

For at least two decades, the army secretly exposed millions of Americans to huge clouds of bacteria and chemical particles. The organisms and particles were sprayed over populated areas to observe their paths, in preparation for an attack by the Soviets with more lethal germs. But while the army was measuring air currents and survivability of the bacteria, no precautions were taken to protect the health and welfare of the millions of people exposed.

Like the other experiments that government agencies had been conducting, the public found out about the germ warfare tests through newspaper accounts in the 1970s. Like the other experiments, these tests were no longer taking place at the time of public disclosure. But unlike the other experiments, germ warfare testing is not merely a matter of history. The possibility of spraying the public again has been left open. An army spokesman testified in 1977 at congressional hearings that the army might resume testing when it finds an "area of vulnerability that takes additional tests."[1] Such an area evidently has been found. A 1986 army report reveals that open air testing is taking place again, at least on a limited basis.[2]

3

Since testing is conducted secretly, we do not know how many people may be exposed, or what plans exist for further testing. Comments and actions by government officials have offered scant comfort. In 1983, spokesmen for the biological warfare laboratories at Fort Detrick, Maryland, would not acknowledge that vulnerability tests were underway, but one official added, "of course we can't tell all of our secrets."

In 1984 the army sought to expand its biological warfare testing facilities in Utah in a manner that seemed intended to draw minimal outside attention. In an apparent effort to avoid congressional hearings, it tried to "reprogram" funds that had been designated for other purposes. When the issue became public, Pentagon officials agreed to a court order to suspend plans pending preparation of an environmental impact statement.

Alexander M. Capron, who served as executive director of the President's Commission on Bioethics, said that under existing rules the army could be spraying over heavily populated areas, and the public would not know.[3] Capron's agency, the only federal commission concerned with ethical problems involving research on humans, was dissolved in 1983.

Compounding the uncertainty is the fact that in 1986 the Reagan administration's budget for chemical and biological warfare exceeded $1 billion, up from $160 million in 1980, although its details were largely secret. The government's interest has been fueled by alleged Soviet violations of treaty commitments. The Soviet Union and the United States signed the 1925 Geneva Protocol that prohibits the use of chemical or biological weapons, and the 1972 Biological Weapons Convention that prohibits the development, production, and stockpiling of biological weapons. Only activities related to prophylactic and defensive measures are permissible.[4]

The administration has claimed that an anthrax epidemic in the Russian city of Sverdlovsk in 1979 was caused by an accidental release of anthrax bacilli that had been illegally stockpiled. It has accused the Soviets and their surrogates of waging war with biological toxins ("yellow rain") in Afghanistan and Southeast Asia. Most recently it said that the Soviet Union is illegally engaged in a program to develop weapons through genetic engineering. All these claims have been challenged by scientific experts, as will be discussed in the course of this study. But the charges have heightened concerns about America's defensive capabilities. Programs have been accelerated to develop vaccines and protective gear. Most significantly, recommendations that had been made in the early 1980s to revitalize the army's open air vulnerability testing program are being carried out.

The Uniqueness of Biological Warfare

Biological weaponry is often lumped with chemical agents, like mustard gas, which was first used with devastating effects in World War I, and nerve gas, which the Soviet Union and the United States currently stockpile in large quantities. Since this book focuses on biological warfare testing, the relationship between the two weapons systems should be clarified. They do have characteristics in common. Their effectiveness would likely depend on meteorological conditions; both are seen as more nasty, terrifying, and uncontrollable than conventional weapons systems. The Pentagon links the two under a single budgetary category, and this also blurs their differences. But beside the distinctive treatment accorded to biological weapons by international treaty, they are unique in other ways.

A biological weapon usually connotes a microorganism used for hostile purposes. Biological agents are generally more potent weight-for-weight than chemical agents because they can reproduce and become more lethal with the passage of time. As an army general who was involved with both systems observed, "chemical agents will cover only tens of square miles, but biological agents can blanket hundreds of thousands of square miles."[5]

If biological agents, such as bacteria or viruses, become established in the environment, they may persist for years. Unlike most chemicals, biological agents cannot be separated from a natural habitat, and they may not be recognized until after they have caused widespread infection. The likelihood of early warning and detection of their presence is virtually nil. Biological weaponry is also much cheaper than other weapons systems. Experts told a United Nations panel in 1969 that "for a large-scale operation against a civilian population, casualties might cost about $2,000 per square kilometer with conventional weapons, $800 with nuclear weapons, $600 with nerve-gas weapons, and $1 with biological weapons."[6]

Thus, biological agents are cheaper and their effects are potentially more insidious, more widespread, longer lasting, and less controllable than those of chemicals. As in nuclear war, there seems to be no genuinely effective defense against a biological warfare attack, especially for a large civilian population. Yet trying to develop one has been part of the rationale behind the army's vulnerability testing program.

Learning about the Tests

Hearings held by the Senate Subcommittee on Health and Scientific Research of the Committee on Human Resources in 1977 revealed the awesome scope of the earlier germ-warfare testing program. Army spokesmen acknowledged that 239 populated areas from coast to coast had been blanketed with bacteria between 1949 and 1969. Tests involved covering areas of Alaska and Hawaii and the cities of San Francisco, Washington, D.C., Key West, and Panama City in Florida. Some tests were more focused, such as those in which bacteria were sprayed onto the Pennsylvania Turnpike or into the New York City subway system.[7]

The hearings further revealed that the incidence of illnesses suddenly increased in some areas near the tests. When Senator Richard Schweiker asked if anyone had been monitoring the health effects on the population in the test areas, army witnesses were momentarily mute. Brigadier General William Augerson finally volunteered that he was unaware of any monitoring system. The army "made an assumption of the innocence of these organisms," he explained.[8]

Distinguished scientists testified at the hearings that the tests were inappropriate and dangerous. They agreed that exposure to heavy concentrations of even apparently innocuous organisms can cause illness. In the words of Dr. J. Mehsen Joseph, director of Laboratories Administration for the Maryland Department of Health and Mental Hygiene, the tests "constituted an unjustifiable health hazard for a particular segment of the population."[9]

Since the army failed to monitor the health of the human population that was targeted during the tests, we shall never know how much disease and death they may have caused. Based on available information and the word of government officials, the public can feel little confidence about protection from resumed outdoor testing. This time, however, because information has become available about previous tests, the public can have a better understanding of the possible consequences.

One important source of information comes from testimony at a trial in 1981. Joined by his family, Edward J. Nevin 3d sued the United States government, alleging that bacteria called *Serratia marcescens*, sprayed by the army over San Francisco in 1950, had killed his grandfather. The trial offered an unusual opportunity to peek behind the veil of secrecy that long had hidden the army's testing program.

The spraying of San Francisco with army bacteria was typical of the secret tests over populated areas that the army conducted for years. The trial brought to light previously classified documents that had lain buried in the tombs of army archives. Former military and scientific officials who had administered the testing program testified that they would be spraying today if still in charge. To gather data for national security, their testimony shows, was their overriding interest. In the process, they overlooked evidence that the tests may have been causing disease.

The officials seemed to have convinced themselves that certain facts were illusory or unimportant, because they did not want to believe them. To be sure, such mind-sets are not unique to biological warfare officials—all human beings are capable of self-delusion and dissimulation. But these characteristics are particularly unsettling when exhibited by authorities whose power can affect the lives of many citizens. Several other incidents in recent history serve as reminders.

Members of the Atomic Energy Commission secretly decided in the 1950s that the public would have to learn to live with radioactive fallout from atomic tests—even though the public had no idea it was being exposed. Similarly, when 6,300 sheep suddenly died in 1968 following chemical warfare tests at the nearby proving ground in Utah, Pentagon spokesmen denied responsibility. Only after prolonged congressional and public pressure for an investigation did the army reverse itself a year later and admit guilt. In another instance, the Public Health Service had been engaged in a 40-year project that involved observing but withholding treatment from syphilitic blacks. After reviewing the propriety of the project, Dr. J. Lawton Smith, a physician-consultant to the Public Health Service, urged in 1969 that the experiment be continued. "You will never have another study like this; take advantage of it," he said.[10]

More recently, members of the Environmental Protection Agency were found to have neglected the agency's mandate to protect the public. They had systematically ignored statutory requirements to control industrial pollution, evidently for political purposes. When the scandal surfaced in 1983, more than twenty of the agency's highest officials, including its director, were forced to resign. Meanwhile, information appears with regularity about newly discovered hazards wrought by miscalculation or wishful thinking of people in authority—from damage caused by acid rain to life-threatening toxic waste dumps; from unsafe nuclear power plants to growing accumulations of radioactive waste with no place for permanent storage.

If one grants even the most honorable motivation to the officials in charge, such incidents reflect the human capability to confuse good intentions with harmful actions. Biological warfare testing may be understood as part of a syndrome in which the welfare of the citizenry can become hostage to this confusion. Whether in the name of national security, ideology, or scientific progress, policies have been implemented that disregard the safety of the American public. In this respect the biological warfare testing program has not been unique. Only in its scope, its exposure of many millions of citizens to army bacteria, did the testing program assume a scale beyond others. Now, because of congressional hearings, the Freedom of Information Act, the Nevin trial, and interviews, a systematic exploration of the issue has become possible. We are able to assess the legacies of the tests and their effects on people. We explore the attitudes of those who were in charge of the biological warfare program in the past, and those in charge today. Such a study tells not only about the testing program, but about this nation's political culture.

The Design of Study

The book is divided into four sections. Part One, comprising this and the following chapter, establishes the setting that led to the first series of tests in the 1950s and 1960s, and to the current interest in renewed outdoor testing. Chapter 2 recalls examples of biological warfare in the past, the development of a United States biological arsenal during World War II, and the rationale of the testing program that began after the war.

Part Two, comprised of Chapters 3 through 6, explores the legacies and legitimacy of the past tests, and raises questions about the appropriateness of resumed open air testing. The section begins with a discussion about Gruinard Island, which remains uninhabitable because of contamination from biological warfare experiments performed four decades earlier. The history and current activities at Fort Detrick are then reviewed, and base officials are cited who maintain that the testing program was and is safe. Chapter 5 reviews the scientific literature, which questions the army's contention that the bacteria used in its tests over populated areas are harmless. The final chapter in the section assesses in detail the spraying of several cities, based on reports of the tests that became available in recent years.

The third section of the book, Chapters 7 and 8, recounts the spraying of San Francisco with germs in 1950, and the 1981 trial brought by the Nevin family in relation to that test. This section lays out documents about the testing program that had not been previously available. It is highlighted by the trial testimony of army officials who ran the germ warfare tests. Their remarks reveal a mind-set that helps explain the urge to test, whether in the past or present.

Part Four, the largest section of the book, bears the most immediate implications. It explores events since 1980 that have led to an expanding biological warfare research program in the United States. Chapters 9 and 10 review the administration's contention that the

Soviet Union is engaged in illegal biological warfare activities. The chapters examine the "yellow rain" issue and the relationship between genetic engineering and the military.

Chapters 11 and 12 survey the army's response to the alleged Soviet violations, particularly as it concerns the issue of testing. As the army enlarges its biological defense program, the push toward extensive testing over populated areas has gathered momentum. Chapter 11 discusses this trend. It cites reports in 1984 and 1985 by government commissions that call for field testing with bacterial and chemical agents to assess detection techniques, and a 1986 army report revealing that such testing is now underway. The book concludes with a discussion of the ethics of spraying unsuspecting citizens with bacteria, and the need for protection against such activities.

To the extent that newspaper investigators, congressional representatives, and citizens like the Nevin family prompted exposure about the earlier tests, they express an essential value of a democratic society. It is in tribute to this spirit, which includes a call for openness about the present program, that we approach the subject of this study.

Notes

1. U.S. Congress: Senate Hearings before the Subcommittee on Health and Scientific Research of the Committee on Human Resources, *Biological Testing Involving Human Subjects by the Department of Defense, 1977*, March 8 and May 23, 1977 (Washington, D.C.: Government Printing Office, 1977), p. 18.

2. U.S. Department of Defense, "Biological Defense Program," Report to the Committee on Appropriations, House of Representatives, Washington, D.C., May 1986 (mimeographed). The report indicates that field testing with microorganisms is now taking place at the Dugway Proving Ground in Utah, although whether elsewhere as well is not made clear. The main purpose of the report was to justify to the Appropriations Committee the army's call for more funds for its expanding biological warfare defense program.

3. Interview, June 2, 1982.

4. The status of biological weaponry and warfare has been reviewed periodically by the Stockholm International Peace Research Institute (SIPRI) since the early 1970s. Its publications include a six-volume series titled *The Problem of Chemical and Biological Warfare* (New York: Humanities Press, 1971–1975). Also see SIPRI, *Weapons of Mass Destruction and the Environment* (London: Taylor & Francis Ltd., 1977); SIPRI, *World Armaments and Disarmament: SIPRI Yearbook 1985* (London: Taylor & Francis Ltd., 1985); SIPRI, *World Armaments and Disarmament: SIPRI Yearbook 1986* (Oxford: Oxford University Press, 1986). The most recent comprehensive treatment of the subject is in Erhard Geissler, ed., *Biological and Toxin Weapons Today* (New York: Oxford University Press, 1986).

5. J. H. Rothschild, Brigadier General, U.S.A. (Ret.), *Tomorrow's Weapons, Chemical and Biological* (New York: McGraw-Hill, 1964), p. 22.

6. Neil C. Livingstone and Joseph D. Douglass, Jr., *CBW: The Poor Man's Atomic Bomb* (Cambridge, Mass.: Institute for Foreign Policy Analysis, 1984), p. 7.

7. Senate Hearings, *Biological Testing,* pp. 125–40.

8. Ibid., p. 19.

9. Ibid., p. 296.

10. These incidents are documented in Leonard A. Cole, *Politics and the Restraint of Science* (Totowa, N.J.: Rowman & Allanheld, 1983), pp. 114, 124–25.

2

Infecting the Enemy

Biological Warfare in the Past, and the Road to Testing

[T]he Tartars, fatigued by such a plague and pestiforous disease, stupefied and amazed, observing themselves dying without hope of health, ordered cadavers placed on their hurling machines and thrown into the city of Caffa, so that by means of these intolerable passengers the defenders died widely. Thus there were projected mountains of dead, nor could the Christians hide or flee, or be freed from such disaster. . . . And soon all the air was infected and the water poisoned, corrupt and putrified, and such a great odor increased. . . . So great and so much was the general mortality that great shouts and clamor arose from Chinese, Indians, Persians, Nubians, Ethiopians, Egyptians, Arabs, Saracens, Greeks, who cried and wept, and suspected the extreme judgment of God.[1]

THUS DID GABRIEL DE MUSSIS describe a biological warfare attack in 1346 on the walled city of Caffa, a seaport on the east coast of the Crimea in south Russia. Now called Feodosia, Caffa was then inhabited largely by merchants and soldiers from the Italian principality of Genoa. The city had been under siege for several years, but the Genoese were holding firm. When the attacking Tartars fell victim to a plague epidemic, their siege weakened, but as de Mussis recounts, they turned their malady into military weaponry. De Mussis was among the "Genoese and Venetian travellers, of whom scarcely 10 survived of 1,000," who were able to flee the city.

Gruesome tales such as this help explain why biological weaponry has been used infrequently—because it has been viewed as more repugnant and less controllable than other weapons systems. Other historical accounts support both notions.

The British reportedly used smallpox as a weapon in colonial America during the French and Indian War. Sir Jeffrey Amherst, commander-in-chief of the British forces, was concerned that his troops west of the Allegheny Mountains were in danger of being overrun by Indians. He wrote to the commander of the garrison at Fort Pitt and urged that smallpox be spread among the disaffected tribes: "You will do well to try to inoculate the Indians by means of blankets as well as to try every other method that can serve to extirpate this exorable race."[2]

Subsequently, in June 1763, Captain Ecuyer of the Royal Americans met with two Indian chiefs under a pretense of friendship and gave them blankets that had been taken from the smallpox hospital. During the following months, according to historians of the episode, many Indians suffered and died as "smallpox raged among the tribes of the Ohio."[3]

In 1942, President Franklin Roosevelt noted that Japan may have been using biological and chemical agents against China. He called such action an "inhuman form of warfare," but approved a secret program to develop a United States capability. While warning the enemy not to initiate gas warfare, he implicitly covered biological agents as well:

> I have been loath to believe that any nation, even our present enemies, could or would be willing to loose upon mankind such terrible and inhumane weapons . . . We promise to pay any perpetrators of such crimes full and swift retaliation in kind, and I feel obliged now to warn the Axis armies and the Axis people in Europe and in Asia that the terrible consequences of any use of these inhumane methods on their part will be brought down swiftly and surely upon their heads.[4]

After World War II, at a Soviet trial concerning Japan's wartime activities, evidence was presented that biological weaponry had been used against China. Eleven Chinese cities had been subjected to attacks with a variety of biological agents. A number of delivery systems had been used, including bombs that dispersed bacteria after exploding and airplanes that dropped feathers and cotton wadding infected with microorganisms. Seven hundred Chinese were victimized by artificially disseminated plague alone.[5]

Japanese Tests on Human Subjects, and the U.S. Reaction

Beside conducting biological warfare, the Japanese engaged in a massive experimental program involving human subjects. The subjects included Chinese, Russians, and "half-breeds," in the words of a Japanese administrator of the program. John Powell, a scholar who obtained reports about the Japanese research under the Freedom of

Information Act in the late 1970s, estimated that at least 3,000 subjects were killed as a result of the experiments. Some died of disease, while others were executed after becoming physical wrecks and unfit for further experimentation.[6]

Although the tests had been known about since the end of World War II, not until Powell obtained the reports did the public learn that experimental subjects included captured American soldiers. As the documents reveal, neither General Shiro Ishii, who was in charge of the program, nor any of his colleagues were tried for their crimes. After the war, the Japanese administrators of the program agreed to provide their American captors with details about the experiments in exchange for their freedom. The documents indicate that the Americans welcomed the arrangement and apparently paid the Japanese for their cooperation.

Dr. Edwin V. Hill, who was chief of Basic Science at Camp Detrick, Maryland, reported in 1947 on his and Dr. Joseph Victor's meeting in Tokyo with Japanese biological warfare experts. Excerpts from his report show the importance that the Americans attached to learning about the Japanese findings, and their desire to protect the perpetrators from punishment:

> Evidence gathered in this investigation has greatly supplemented and amplified previous aspects of this field. It represents data which have been obtained by Japanese scientists at the expenditure of many millions of dollars and years of work. Information has accrued with respect to human susceptibility to those diseases as indicated by specific infectious doses of bacteria. Such information could not be obtained in our own laboratories because of scruples attached to human experimentation. These data were secured with a total outlay of 250,000 Yen to date, a mere pittance compared with the actual cost of the studies.
>
> Furthermore, the pathological material which has been collected constitutes the only material evidence of the nature of these experiments. It is hoped that individuals who voluntarily contributed this information will be spared embarrassment because of it and that every effort will be taken to prevent this information from falling into other hands.[7]

A 1947 memorandum by Dr. Edward Wetter and Mr. H. I. Stubblefield was circulated among military and State Department officials, and spoke directly to the question of how to treat the Japanese. It urged that since General Ishii and his colleagues were cooperating with the Americans, they should not be treated as war criminals: "The value to U.S. of Japanese BW data is of such importance to national security as to far outweigh the value accruing from war crimes prosecution."[8]

The ethics of the Japanese actions disturbed some of the American authorities, but not because they were concerned that the Japanese would escape punishment. Instead, they were interested in figuring out how to avoid the ethical issue and to obtain the information. At the time that America's biological warfare authorities were exchanging these memoranda, Nazi scientists were being tried in Nuremberg for similarly barbaric experimentation on human subjects. One member of the State, War, Navy Coordinating Committee, Cecil F. Hubbert, noted that such "experiments on human beings . . . have been condemned as war crimes by the International Military Tribunal." Yet Hubbert recommended that none of the members of the Japanese biological warfare group be prosecuted for war crimes, and that the information they provided be kept secret.

In a memorandum written with E. F. Lyons, Jr., of the Plans and Policy Section of the War Crimes Branch, Hubbert indicated that "the Japanese BW group is the only known source of data from scientifically controlled experiments showing direct effects of BW agents on humans." He suggested that the United States government take the false position that "the data on hand . . . does [sic] not appear sufficient at this time to constitute a basis for sustaining war crimes charge against Ishii and/or his associates."[9]

No Japanese were ever indicted or tried for crimes related to biological warfare activities.

Toward Testing in the United States

United States interest in biological warfare began two months before the Japanese attacked Pearl Harbor. Secretary of War Henry Stimson asked the National Academy of Sciences to evaluate the subject, and a committee appointed by the academy concluded that biological warfare was feasible. In 1942 President Roosevelt approved the establishment of a biological warfare program. Later that year, responsibility for research and development was given to the army's Chemical Warfare Service.[10]

Before the end of World War II, the United States and Great Britain had worked cooperatively to amass huge arsenals of biological weapons that could unleash diseases such as anthrax and brucellosis (undulant fever). Despite the Allies' posture that they would never be the first to use germ weaponry, the possibility remained open. Long after it was clear that Germany and Japan had become unable to mount such an attack, the Allied build-up of biological weapons continued. The rationale for considering first use was akin to that for dropping the atomic bombs on Japan—to shorten the war.[11]

In fact, as a memorandum from the office of the Chief of the

Chemical Corps in 1950 indicates, preparations for using plant-growth inhibitors were underway when the war ended. "Had the war continued a few months longer," the report says, "it is believed that these agents would have found actual employment, at least on a small scale, in the Pacific area."[12]

After the war, the American biological warfare program was cut back, although the public was not aware that the United States even had a program. In January 1946 George W. Merck, of the Merck Pharmaceutical Company, issued a press release on behalf of the War Department that first disclosed the American effort. Merck was a consultant to the Secretary of War on biological warfare and had worked on the program throughout the war. The program, he revealed, included research, testing, development, and production of biological agents, all conducted in the "strictest secrecy."[13] Although the nation was demobilizing, Merck admonished the government to maintain a strong biological warfare program: "Work in this field, born of the necessity of war, cannot be ignored in time of peace; it must be continued on a sufficient scale to provide an adequate defense."[14] His recommendation did not go unheeded.

BW Testing over Populated Areas

Although the arms budget remained modest in the postwar years, suspicion about Soviet military intentions was growing. In 1948 the Research and Development Board of the office of the Secretary of Defense requested an evaluation of biological weapons as a means of sabotage. A Committee on Biological Warfare was established under the chairmanship of Ira L. Baldwin. On October 5th the Baldwin Committee issued a report "assessing the potentialities and capabilities of biological warfare as a subversive weapon."[15] In this report lie the rationale and authority for the open air tests that took place in populated areas during the following decades.

The Baldwin report focused on an aspect of biological warfare that previously had received scant attention. Titled "Report on Special BW Operations," its emphasis lay on the covert and subversive possibilities of biological warfare. It concluded that the United States was particularly susceptible to covert attack with biological agents, and that "the current biological warfare research and development program is not now authorized to meet the requirements necessary to prepare defensive measures against special BW operations." The report recommended the pursuit of several goals, including the development of means to detect biological warfare agents, development of methods of decontamination and protection, and the assessment of methods for dissemination of biological agents.[16]

Among suggested research projects was one that provided the basis for the open air experimental program: "Test ventillating systems, subway systems, and water supply systems with innocuous organisms to determine quantitatively the extent to which such subversive dissemination of pathogenic biological agents is possible."[17] This proposal was the genesis for later large-scale testing over populated areas. It remains a source of justification for the army's claim that testing is still necessary to assess vulnerability to enemy attack. In the words of the report:

> Biological agents would appear to be well adapted to subversive use since very small amounts of such agents can be effective. A significant portion of the human population within selected target areas may be killed or incapacitated. The food supply of the nation could be depleted to an extent which materially would reduce the nation's capacity to defend itself and to wage war. Serious outbreaks of disease of man, animals or plants also would result in profound psychological disturbances.[18]

Although these words were written in 1948, America's vulnerability to biological warfare seems little different today. Nothing in the public record suggests that the millions of dollars spent on tests, or the risks to millions of citizens exposed to bacterial and chemical agents, have lessened the problems mentioned in the report. A study conducted in 1984 at the army's request by the National Academy of Sciences' Army Board on Science and Technology determined that U.S. troops and civilians might not even know if they were under biological attack. Not only does the United States now lack sufficient chemical and biological sensing equipment, according to the study, but under existing plans for development none could be anticipated to be effective in the future.[19] The 1984 report called for "realistic operational testing" and "field exercises" in hopes of developing such equipment.[20]

Thus, after decades of testing with biological agents in simulated attacks, we still have no adequate sensing devices, let alone a means to protect the population. The 1984 army report repeats the concerns expressed in the 1948 Baldwin report about America's vulnerability to biological warfare attack. The message is disquieting to those concerned about resumed secret spraying.

The newer report emphasizes that "the problem of inadequate testing of detection devices, particularly those for actual agents, should be addressed."[21] It urges that open air testing and training exercises be implemented using "realistic, nontoxic simulants," words that could as well have appeared in the 1948 Baldwin report.

The rationale for more research and development in the 1984 report is similar to that in the Baldwin report written 36 years earlier. Among the conclusions in 1948: "1) Biological agents would appear to be well adapted to subversive use. 2) The United States is peculiarly susceptible to attack by special BW operations. 3) The subversive use of biological agents by a potential enemy prior to declaration of war presents a grave danger to the United States."[22]

Several of the diseases in the 1948 list could be "produced by some possible BW agents" and are evidently equally threatening today. Tularemia, anthrax, and brucellosis, whatever our advances in treatment capabilities, could still debilitate or kill masses of exposed citizens. We seem just as vulnerable to methods of delivery now as in 1948, as is made clear in the 1984 assessment. The population is no better protected now against attack by water contamination, food and beverage contamination, aerosols, or direct infection. As if anticipating the 1984 report, an army brochure issued a year earlier confirms that many of the diseases that were considered biological warfare threats forty years ago remain threats against which defensive measures are still being sought.[23]

The impression gained from any reasonable assessment of the United States biological warfare programs, past or present, is that unless the type of agent and means of dissemination are known in advance, there can be virtually no protection for an exposed population. Yet as a 1986 army report reveals, open air testing has been resumed.[24] Whether or not the army will be testing in heavily populated areas is not clear. Since such tests are conducted secretly, people have no way of knowing whether and when they are being used as experimental subjects. No monitoring of the health of the affected population took place in the past, and there is no evidence that the army's approach to the issue has changed.

Thus, the nature of past vulnerability tests is not only of academic interest. It raises questions about how such testing is being conducted today. We must wonder if the mind-set of the contemporary biological warfare establishment resembles that of the past, when the quest for information appeared to supersede considerations about health and safety. This mind-set allowed American officials to arrange that Japanese scientists who killed human subjects in biological warfare experiments not be "embarrassed." At the same time these officials were sponsoring tests that exposed millions of unwitting Americans to bacteria and chemical particles.

The bacteria that were used as testing agents can be divided into three categories: those known to cause harm to humans, those assumed to be harmless, and those that initially were thought to be innocuous but, as testing continued, raised suspicions that they were causing disease.

Simulated Attacks

Beginning in the late 1940s and for a "total period of several years," according to Dr. R. G. H. Watson, director of the British Chemical Defense Establishment in 1981, the United States, Canada, and Britain cooperated in spraying pathogens in the area of the Bahama Islands in the Caribbean. Details of the tests are still secret, but they involved highly virulent organisms. Thousands of animals died as a result of the tests. Although Watson does not refer to human victims, he mentions the death of "major animal species" including guinea pigs, mice, rabbits, and monkeys.[25]

A report from the office of the chief of the U.S. Army's Chemical Corps in 1950 confirmed the cooperative effort of the United States with the British in the testing of "BW anti-personnel agents . . . in the Caribbean area." The report called for "further field tests on a realistic scale so it will be possible to assess the full potentialities of BW and develop the most effective methods for its employment on an operational scale."[26]

Areas in the Bahamas that were heavily populated with humans may not have been intentionally exposed to deadly bacteria. Nevertheless, even if bacterial sprays were aimed elsewhere, wind shifts and human miscalculation could have brought virulent organisms into contact with people. This would be consistent with other army tests that endangered unsuspecting populations. Such incidents occurred when radioactive particles from nuclear weapons tests drifted beyond control, or when unexpected wind currents wafted nerve gas over areas populated with humans and animals. The same could be expected from bacterial clouds.

Beyond the tests in the Bahamas in which bacteria known to be very dangerous were used, there is suggestive evidence that unsuspecting human populations in the United States were also exposed to well-known pathogens and toxins. Documents were uncovered in 1979 indicating that the Central Intelligence Agency had obtained quantities of *Hemophilus pertussis,* the whooping-cough bacteria, from Fort Detrick in March 1955. The agency then engaged in field testing with bacterial agents along Florida's Gulf Coast. According to the state's medical records, the incidence of whooping cough in Florida tripled that year compared to the previous year, from 339 cases and one death in 1954 to 1080 and twelve deaths in 1955.[27]

During the 1960s, as other documents revealed, the army released various gases and hallucinogenic drugs in open air tests in Maryland and Utah. Thousands of soldiers were exposed. Shortly after reports about the tests were uncovered in 1979, the army announced that it would try to contact the victims to see if there were long-term effects.[28] Nothing has been heard from the army about the matter since then.

These tests involved biological, chemical, and radioactive agents known to be virulent and toxic. Many more people, perhaps tens of millions, were exposed to bacterial and chemical agents that the army alleged, and continues to allege, were harmless. These so-called simulants of pathogenic bacteria have been sprayed in every region of the United States, from coast to coast, over cities, in buildings, on roads, and in tunnels. The medical literature at the time of the tests, as will be shown later, raised questions about the safety of each of the simulants used. Nevertheless, the United States government continues to dispute evidence that its simulant agents ever caused disease. Indeed, some of the same agents are being used in the army's current open air tests.[29]

The history of germ warfare testing has involved not only deception of the public, but self-deception and miscalculation on the part of the administrators. The consequences of some tests still stand as reminders of this fact. None is more striking than the legacy of Britain's Gruinard Island.

Notes

1. Vincent J. Derbes, "De Mussis and the Great Plague of 1348," *Journal of the American Medical Association,* 196, no. 1 (April 4, 1966): 60.

2. E. Wagner Stearn and Allen E. Stearn, *The Effect of Smallpox on the Destiny of the Amerindian* (Boston: Bruce Humphries Publishers, 1945), pp. 44–55.

3. Ibid.

4. Robert Harris and Jeremy Paxman, *A Higher Form of Killing* (New York: Hill & Wang, 1982), p. 118.

5. John W. Powell, "A Hidden Chapter in History," *Bulletin of the Atomic Scientists* 37, no. 8 (October 1981): 45–49.

6. John W. Powell, "Japan's Germ Warfare: The U.S. Coverup of a War Crime," *Bulletin of Concerned Asian Scholars* 12, no. 4 (1980): 3.

7. Ibid., p. 10.

8. Powell, "A Hidden Chapter in History," p. 48.

9. Ibid.

10. "U.S. Army Activity in the U.S. Biological Warfare Programs," Vol. 1, February 1977, included in U.S. Congress. Senate Hearings before the Subcommittee on Health and Scientific Research of the Committee on Human Resources, *Biological Testing Involving Human Subjects by the Department*

of Defense, 1977, March 8 and May 23, 1977 (Washington, D.C. Government Printing Office, 1977), pp. 26–27.

11. Harris and Paxman, *A Higher Form of Killing,* pp. 105–6.

12. Top Secret Report by Colonel William M. Creasy, Chief, Research and Engineering Division, Office of the Chief, Chemical Corps, U.S. Army, February 25, 1950, p. 2. Although the agents are not named in the report, they are probably like the defoliants later used by the United States during the Vietnam War. Such agents were unequivocally understood by the army to be biological warfare weapons, as Creasy's report makes clear: "Biological warfare is the military employment of living organisms (bacteria, viruses, rickettsia, fungi), their toxic products, or chemical plant growth regulators to produce death or casualties of man, animals, or plants" (p. 3).

13. George W. Merck, Special Consultant for Biological Warfare, "Report to the Secretary of War," January 3, 1946, in Senate Hearings, *Biological Testing,* p. 68.

14. Ibid., p. 71.

15. I. L. Baldwin, Chairman, Committee on Biological Warfare, "Report on Special BW Operations," Memorandum for the Research and Development Board of the National Military Establishment, Washington, D.C., October 5, 1948, p. i.

16. Ibid, pp. i, 5.

17. Ibid., p. 7.

18. Ibid., p. 3.

19. *New York Times,* August 16, 1984, p. A-13.

20. *Assessment of Chemical and Biological Sensor Technologies,* A Report by the Committee on Chemical and Biological Sensor Technologies, Board on Army Science and Technology, National Research Council of the National Academy of Sciences (Washington, D.C.: National Academy Press, 1984), pp. 8–9.

21. Ibid., p. 70.

22. Baldwin, "Report on Special BW Operations," p. 7.

23. "USAMRIID: Respected Worldwide for Research," in *Fort Detrick,* U.S. Army Health Services Command (circa. 1983), pp. 6–7.

24. U.S. Department of Defense, "Biological Defense Program," Report to the Committee on Appropriations, House of Representatives, Washington, D.C., May 1986, ch. 1, p. 10 (mimeographed).

25. Letter to Jeremy Paxman from Dr. R. G. H. Watson, Director, Chemical Defense Establishment, Porton Down, U.K., June 16, 1981.

26. Creasy, in Top Secret Report, p. 33.

27. *International Herald Tribune,* December 18, 1979.

28. *Army Times,* November 19, 1979.

29. "Biological Defense Program," ch. 1, pp. 10–11.

PART TWO
TESTS AND LEGACIES

3

Living near Gruinard Island

TWO HOURS FROM Inverness by car, past the majestic peaks of the Highlands, the northwest coast of Scotland comes into view. A promontory is rounded, and Gruinard Island appears in the distance. An island of greens and browns, it is the centerpiece of a breathtaking panorama framed by the cliffs and heather of the mainland.

The sun is high in summer, and people are bathing off the shore of the mainland. An occasional boat passes, but none moves toward the island. Since World War II, when British and American scientists conducted biological warfare experiments there, no one has been permitted to land. Gruinard Island remains contaminated with anthrax spores that were used in tests more than forty years ago. The danger to humans and livestock remains undiminished and may persist for centuries; no one knows for sure.[1] Like a Pacific atoll that remains contaminated after nuclear weapons tests, Gruinard has been made unfit for human habitation. Unlike a distant Pacific island, however, Gruinard stands in constant view of villagers and tourists, an ever-visible monument to scientific miscalculation. It lies across the bay two miles from slopes filled with grazing sheep, an area of scenic beauty that attracts visitors from around the world.

As Gruinard Island is approached by boat, its hues sharpen into rock and rich low foliage. A trip around the island's four-mile perimeter reveals a variety of textures. Off the northern shore, forbidding stone walls jut from the water. The island's graceful hills are gilded by scrub and stone, and on the western face a small cluster of trees stands above the shore line. Beneath the shrubbery lies a picturesque beach whose coast is etched by pools and eddies.

A surprising variety of birds swoop toward the rocky ledges. Far below the silhouettes of perched gulls and cormorants, a seal's head bobs above the waves. A single stone hut remains on the western slope of the island, a reminder of a time when crofters—small farmers—lived and worked there. The hut purportedly contains gear belonging to government scientists who take measurements periodically to confirm the island's continued infectivity. The anthrax spores have settled beneath the topsoil. As long as the surface is not disturbed, there seems little risk that the island's aviary inhabitants will become infected or carry the deadly cargo to the mainland.

The only evidence of recent human activity appears in the form of signs posted every few hundred yards along the coastal edge:

GRUINARD ISLAND

THIS ISLAND IS

GOVERNMENT PROPERTY UNDER EXPERIMENT.

THE GROUND IS CONTAMINATED WITH ANTHRAX

AND DANGEROUS.

LANDING IS PROHIBITED

BY ORDER 1983.

The plates bearing the year's digits are lightly fastened so that they may be replaced annually.

The Tests on Gruinard Island

At the beginning of World War II, in response to fears that Germany and Japan had developed biological weapons, Britain, like the United States, began a biological warfare program. In 1941 several scientists embarked on a secret project involving the development of anthrax spores for military use. Gruinard Island was chosen as the site to assess the lethality of the spores after their release by explosive devices. Sheep were tethered at measured distances from a central point, as one of the men who participated recalls. Allen Younger, then a major in the Royal Engineers, explains his role in setting up the first experiment. "They asked me to help load the weapon," Younger says. A scientist poured a gruel containing billions of anthrax spores into a container "which I held nervously. I'd been told just how toxic this stuff was, and I knew that if I'd inhaled even the tiniest bit, that would have been it."[2]

When the scientists and crew were safely distant, the cannister was exploded and anthrax spores wafted about. The next day the sheep began to die. Anthrax-infested carcasses soon littered the site. Dressed in protective clothing, the scientists returned to investigate. Soldiers were brought to the island to help dispose of the contaminated sheep by heaving them over a cliff, burying them under rocks, and then detonating the area with explosives. To avoid carrying infection to the mainland, the scientists' and soldiers' protective gear was removed and burned at the edge of the contaminated zone. Tests on the island involving anthrax weapons were ended in 1943.

The experiments helped in the development of a vast arsenal of anthrax bombs by Britain and the United States. But the program led to unexpected consequences. The scientists had chosen Gruinard as the experimental site in the belief that the mainland would be safe from contamination. They assumed that any spores drifting beyond the island would be dispersed and settle into the surrounding water, where they would not survive. As an additional precaution experiments were conducted when the wind was blowing from the mainland toward the sea. Nevertheless, about the time the tests were ended, anthrax broke out in a mainland hamlet across the bay. Sheep and other livestock became infected and died. Although the nature of the Gruinard experiments remained secret to the local community, the government tacitly assumed responsibility for the anthrax deaths by compensating the owners of the dead animals. Whether the mainland infections were caused by unexpected winds or by an infected carcass that floated to the mainland remains uncertain. But the incident was viewed as a crisis at Porton Down, Britain's chemical and biological warfare center.[3]

Another miscalculation involved the difficulty in ridding the island of anthrax spores. Following the outbreak of anthrax on the mainland, Younger and Dr. Paul Fildes, an eminent scientist who was in charge of Britain's biological warfare program, returned to the island to rid it of contamination. "Our plan was to burn the heather off the island and help destroy the anthrax spores," says Younger. They started a fire. "The island was very dry, and that night all the island seemed to be aflame. There was a dense cloud of smoke heading toward the southwest, and a line of fire ate its way up the side of the island."[4]

When other scientists later returned to evaluate the effects of burning the entire island, they must have been stunned. Contamination with anthrax spores seemed as widespread as before. The experiments had left a forbidding legacy that would continue for generations, and it was apparent that the scientists who fathered the tests had made a monumental misjudgment. "I doubt that we would do such an experiment now if we had to in those conditions," says the current director of Porton Down.[5]

Local Residents

During the years that Gruinard Island has been contaminated, few of the mainland residents have shown overt apprehension.[6] The mood is typified by Duncan MacLellan, who runs the post office in the village of Laide across from the island. Barely a toddler when the experiments were carried out, he has always lived within view of the island. "I guess I figure I have been here for forty years and nothing has happened—at least as far as I know. So I just don't think much about it."

The beauty of the area continues to attract new residents, who dismiss concerns about the island. Steven MacDonald and his wife moved to Laide a few years ago to raise their young family. Their house sits atop a point that offers a magnificent view of the bay, the island, and the surrounding peaks of the mainland. "We used to vacation here and enjoyed it so much we decided to move permanently. It is the most beautiful place I have ever seen in Scotland," MacDonald says. Not 200 yards from the MacDonald home, down the road to the jetty, a sign warns that Gruinard Island across the bay is contaminated with anthrax and must not be approached. MacDonald did consider the matter before moving, but felt the island posed no problem for him and his family. He says, cryptically, that he is not sure the island is really dangerous, and that "the government may have other motives for keeping people away." He does not elaborate.

It is unclear how representative MacLellan's and MacDonald's lack of concern is among the local population. In recent years several have voiced their worries publicly and begun to seek remedial action by the government. The burgeoning concerns are perhaps best expressed by a few lifelong residents of the area. Ann Munro, eighty years old, was for most of her life the elementary school teacher at Laide. Miss Munro visited the island many times in the 1920s and 1930s. Her father owned sheep and cattle, some of which grazed there under the care of a crofter. "My father knew the history of the people who lived there and had been evicted. There were several families living on the island, some with many children." Sportsmen would venture to the island, she recalls, and others would go there to relax and picnic. "It's a very attractive island actually, a beautiful place.

"Then the news came during the war that it was to be used for an experiment on the destruction of animals," Miss Munro says. "I remember a man coming around and asking my father if he would sell sheep for it. He said he would not. He would not send any sheep to be destroyed. At the time, my father was seventy, and he was loyal to the extreme as far as government or royalty were concerned. But I can remember that he was really angry at what was done. He thought it was a crime. I think I was more against it than some others because my father was so much against it, and this helped me realize it was a horrible thing."

The continued contamination of the island has reinforced Miss Munro's suspicions about the government's motives. She tells of an encounter a few years ago with government scientists who were staying in a small hotel across the road from her home. "I happened to be strolling nearby and some of them stopped and talked to me. They said, 'We're investigating all these myths about Gruinard Island.' I said, 'What myths?' 'Oh, that there was anthrax there, and that cattle were destroyed by the anthrax.' I said, 'That's not a myth. I remember the day very well when anthrax was discovered on the mainland, and I know the names of all the people that lost their horses and cattle.'

"Whether they were testing me or not I don't know," Miss Munro says. "But they made out it was a myth, and that there was no harm from anything that was put on the island." Miss Munro is gentle but direct. She is indignant that the government scientists tried to toy with her. She fixes her eyes on the listener. "What I tell you is not hearsay. It's what I know from experience. I taught at Laide. The island was opposite me."

John Alec Macrea was born nearby, and as a child was taught by Miss Munro. At 48 he is lean and ruggedly handsome. For twelve years he was a naval officer and worked as an electronics expert on the defense early warning systems in Canada and the United States. He retired in 1971 and returned to the Gruinard area to enter the building business with his brother. John Alec, as he is called in the community, is widely respected for his intelligence and sincerity. He is very religious, and more than one neighbor cautioned against trying to visit John Alec on a Sunday.

Although in the mid-1980s Macrea had become a leader among local residents concerned about Gruinard, for most of his life he paid little heed to the island. "I attended the Laide school at the time of the experiments, but was totally unaware of their significance," Macrea says. "Actually it was not until a few years ago that my interest was raised. There was a chap named Gwynne Roberts who did a feature on Gruinard Island in the *Times* weekend magazine. He interviewed various experts on biological and chemical warfare, and I ended up gleaning information from him when he came here. Since then other members of the media have come to the area and shown interest, and this has made me much more aware of the degree of contamination and the unique situation we have on our doorstep."

Macrea has informed himself about anthrax and the Gruinard tests. He has asked several government officials about the possibility of decontaminating the island, and is convinced that successive governments have paid little attention because the project would be very expensive. Money is spent only for "more politically weighted projects," he says. "I personally believe cost should not enter into it,

because given the right conditions one could breed a second generation of spores. Porton Down scientists have been getting higher spore
counts at test points that they have previously made counts at. I think
there is concern there. This could be a time bomb. It has got the
potential."

Macrea outlines his scientific understanding of the problem: "The
spores remain in suspended animation until given the right incubation conditions. They're just waiting for the opportunity for self-
preservation like any living organism. The fact that things appear to
have remained dormant for years is no guarantee that a climatic
change or dead animal couldn't affect all that. If the weather remained warm for a period, or if an animal died in the contaminated
area and its blood became available, the right conditions will be there
to set the process in motion." The process that Macrea refers to
involves the transformation of a spore into its vegetative state. The
anthrax bacillus then becomes actively hazardous and capable of
rapid reproduction.

Macrea discussed this process with other local residents. While
many now share his concern, he admits to frustration when some
insist that they do not want to create any disturbances. "Some of the
locals have said that the situation has not resulted in any detriment to
the community. I am not prepared to believe that statement because I
understand that even a mild contact of anthrax can result in influ-
enza-type symptoms. . . . For somebody to glibly say that the community has not suffered—well, there is no research that's been carried
out to the best of my knowledge. . . . The community was virtually
nonexistent as far as the authorities were concerned when these
experiments were carried out."

Macrea recounts with a mixture of satisfaction and annoyance an
effort the previous year to gather support for a petition to the
government. He sought endorsement to a list of concerns that he
intended to present to officials. He was pleased with the community's
response, but chagrined by the government's. The petition sought
answers from the government to three questions: whether experiments were still being carried out on Gruinard Island; whether the
island was being retained for future experiments; and whether there
were any intentions to decontaminate it.

Macrea left the petition on a counter at the post office in Laide and
made no effort to canvass for signatures. Within a few days seventy
people had signed. Macrea interpreted the response as an indication
of a solid base of concern. Many more would have signed, he believes,
but the police confiscated the petition. Macrea feels the police action
was at the behest of the national government, which has consistently

tried to minimize publicity about Gruinard. The action reinforced Macrea's doubts that the government is interested in solving the problem. In seeking signatures, "we had not violated any government law or regulation," Macrea says. "We weren't involved in any subversive activity. We had every right to air our opinion." Macrea later met with his parliamentary representative and other officials, but feels that none is committed to finding a solution. He is cynical about recurring reports that the government soon hopes to clean the island.

In fact, Macrea may be holding a mistaken premise. The government probably wants to decontaminate Gruinard, but the task may be virtually impossible. The reasons for the government's wish seem obvious. Not only is the island a potential source of danger to humans and livestock, but it remains a continuing political embarrassment. In recent years, as the media have increasingly focused on Gruinard, the government has drawn more criticism. An incident associated with the issue raised near-hysteria in October 1981. Protesters notified newspapers that they had deposited anthrax-infested soil from Gruinard at the Chemical Defense Establishment at Porton Down, and at Blackpool Tower where the annual Conservative Party conference was being held. A government spokesman despaired that the action "put the whole country at danger," while the Department of Health described it as "incredibly irresponsible."[7]

A month later a news report indicated that Porton Down scientists would undertake a review of possible decontamination methods.[8] Then, in July 1982, the Ministry of Defense said it was planning field trials of methods for decontamination. While some expressed relief that the government seemed to be trying to solve the problem, others remained skeptical. John Alec Macrea recalls several such reports. "They seem to come up on an annual basis. The government must have a rotary system where all of a sudden around comes Gruinard Island, and they put a little snippet in the paper to make people assume that a great deal is being done. But I wonder just how much is being done."

Several proposals for decontamination have been offered over the years. They include encasing the island in cement, stripping off the top layer of soil and dumping it into the Atlantic, neutralizing the spores with steam or chemicals, or bombarding them with radiation.[9] All the ideas were rejected as impractical or unlikely to succeed. Another suggestion, in contrast to the supposed aim of decontaminating the island, came in 1981 from a Member of Parliament, who proposed using the island as a dump for nuclear waste. His suggestion outraged many of the area's residents, and the councils of two nearby villages expressed opposition.[10] Although the idea was withdrawn, this confusion of official signals has contributed to the doubts harbored by Macrea and others.

In addition to contamination of the island, Macrea believes the area is faced with another problem. He recounts how the mainland suffered the anthrax outbreak at the time of the tests. "The dead animals on the mainland were buried without any precautions whatsoever," he says, based on his own recollections as well as conversations with others who remember the episode. "The owners just dug a hole and stuck them in the ground." Macrea continues: "So not only should we be concerned about Gruinard Island, but we should be concerned about a particular spot on the mainland that has been used by campers. It is an open piece of ground and I am convinced that we have got a major source of contamination there." Macrea believes the government has not taken soil samples nor monitored local residents' health, to prevent embarrassment from the attendant publicity.

Whether Macrea's fears are exaggerated, whether the government will attempt to decontaminate the Gruinard area, or even whether the island *can* be decontaminated, may be answered in the next few years. But remarks by Dr. Rex Watson, the present director of Porton Down, give pause. He said that scientists now at Porton Down "expect there to be an area of contamination for the next tens, perhaps even hundreds of years."[11] In an implicit suggestion that no amount of funding or effort can clean up such a large anthrax contaminated area, Dr. Watson remarked that if Berlin had been bombarded with anthrax weapons in 1945, it would still be uninhabitable today.[12]

Notes

1. Although the tests were under British auspices, six American bacteriologists worked with the British team. "We'd go over to the island every day and work over there because we had set up apparatus that held the sampling devices and all that sort of thing," recalled Dr. William B. Sarles, one of the Americans. Sarles was later decorated by both the United States and Great Britain for his wartime work on biological weapons. Transcript, "NBC Magazine," NBC Television Network, National Broadcasting Company, May 15, 1983, p. 16.

2. Gwynne Roberts, "The Deadly Legacy of Anthrax Island," *The Sunday Times Magazine* (London), February 15, 1981, p. 23.

3. Ibid.

4. Ibid.

5. Robert Harris and Jeremy Paxman, *A Higher Form of Killing* (New York: Hill & Wang, 1982), p. 73.

6. Interviews with local residents were conducted in July 1983.

7. Statements were reported in David Nicholson-Lord, "Anthrax Protest

'Puts Whole Country at Risk'," *The Times* (London), October 12, 1981, p. 26. Additional related stories were in October 14, 1981, p. 2, and October 15, 1981, p. 2.

   8. *The Times* (London), December 2, 1981, p. 5.
   9. Ibid., October 12, 1981, p. 26, and December 2, 1981, p. 5.
   10. Roberts, "The Deadly Legacy," p. 27.
   11. Harris and Paxman, *A Higher Form of Killing*, p. 73.
   12. Nicholson-Lord, "Anthrax Protest," p. 26. In 1987, the British Ministry of Defense declared that the island had been decontaminated, but many observers remained skeptical. "No matter how many samples are taken and analysed, how many optimistic statements are issued by the ministry, it will take Gruinard Island a few generations to shed its sinister aura," wrote Donald Macleod in *The Scotsman Magazine* 8, no. 1 (April 1987):17.

4

Fort Detrick's Mysteries

THREE THOUSAND MILES from Gruinard Island, fifty miles from Washington, D. C., lies the quaint town of Frederick, Maryland. The road to town, as a local tourism pamphlet says, bends through "gracefully contoured countryside." But the pamphlet's claim that the town symbolizes "all that is noble in America's heritage and promising in its future" might prompt some disagreement.

The northwest border of Frederick abuts Fort Detrick, the site of the U.S. Army's biological warfare headquarters. Since 1969, when the United States declared an end to its offensive biological warfare program, the American effort has been sharply limited. Some of the base's buildings are now used for cancer research, while others remain devoted to defensive biological warfare work. A few remain, in the local vernacular, "hot spots." They are off-limits to human beings for the same reason that Gruinard Island is: contamination with pathogens or toxins.

Among the most imposing structures at Fort Detrick is a seven-story building, taller than any other on the base. The building, unpretentiously numbered 470 but known as "the Tower," is visible from almost any point on the base. It stands as a constant reminder of what Fort Detrick had been dedicated to. The Tower has been bolted shut since the 1960s, and on its front door is an innocuous sign: "ALL VISITORS—MAINT. PERSONNEL REPORT TO SECRETARY OFF. ROOM 201 TO SIGN REGISTOR [sic] WHEN ENTERING OR LEAVING BUILDING." In fact, since the 1960s no one has entered or left this building except monitors in protective clothing, who periodically confirm that the building remains contaminated with anthrax spores. It is America's Gruinard Island.

From a distance, the Tower appears to be a normal office building, perhaps a storage facility. But behind its red brick walls and painted-over windows are no separate floors or stories. Instead, filling its length is a giant metal vat in which bacteria were grown in huge quantities. At the base lies a large propeller that had been used to stir slurries of bacteria. Along the tank's sides is a grating network that enables technicians to reach different levels.

Other locations at the base have been decontaminated by forcing formaldehyde under pressure into the enclosed sections that contained the unwanted germs. But according to a scientist who works at Fort Detrick, because the inside of the Tower is unpartitioned, formaldehyde cannot be forced under sufficient pressure to decontaminate the upper reaches of the facility. Even so, since the contaminated areas are enclosed by the building's outer walls, it seems possible that a major effort could decontaminate the Tower. But short of considerable funding and effort, no one knows when the building will be safe to enter or how much longer it will cast its shadow over the "gracefully contoured countryside."

History

Fort Detrick's biological weapons history began with American concern that Germany and Japan might be developing biological weaponry. In 1942, under presidential directive, Secretary of War Harold Stimson created the War Research Service (WRS) to oversee the establishment of an American biological warfare program. The WRS was headed by George W. Merck, president of the Merck Pharmaceutical Company, and its function was kept secret. The agency was nominally attached to the civilian Federal Security Agency, whose responsibility was to "promote social and economic security, advance educational opportunities and promote public health."[1]

The following year, at the request of the WRS, the Army Chemical Warfare Service started construction of specially designed laboratories and pilot plants at Detrick Field, a small National Guard airfield on the edge of Frederick, Maryland. Security and secrecy at Camp Detrick, as the base was then called, were as stringent as for the Manhattan Project. The site grew to become the nation's principal research and development center for biological warfare. But not until 1946, four months after the war had formally ended, did the public learn that the United States had a biological warfare program.

The wartime effort demonstrated the virtual unity of offensive and defensive research. The army's official history of Fort Detrick, written in 1968, indicated that "research and development in the offensive aspects of BW proceeded hand in hand with defensive developments for, in truth, the two are almost inseparable."[2] The army must wish this clause had never been printed, since the government's position now is that America is engaged only in defensive research.

In any case, the effort during the war was very broad, ranging from the development of effective microorganisms to the munitions that would deliver them. Questions were investigated about the mechanism for transmitting disease—whether by way of the respiratory tract, digestive system, or open wounds—through methods of growing microorganisms and determining the ideal size of infectious particles.[3] The difficulty of establishing a defense against biological weaponry was expressed in the army's recognition that field masks for protection against gases were one million times less efficient than would be necessary to filter out biological particles.[4]

In January 1946, when the War Department informed the public about the biological warfare program, it released a report by George Merck about the work done at Detrick. Merck mentioned the program's effort to make bacteria more virulent and at the same time try to control their infectivity. Once again the indistinguishability between offensive and defensive research was cited: "While the main objective in all these endeavors was to develop methods for defending ourselves against possible enemy use of biological warfare agents, it was necessary to investigate offensive possibilities in order to learn what measures could be used for defense."[5] This linkage was commonly understood to be indissoluble, and the official position for the next twenty-five years. Critics of today's defensive program believe the linkage continues to be unavoidable, despite the army's attempt to revise its earlier position.

Immediately after the war, the chief of the Chemical Warfare Service became responsible for continuing biological warfare research at Detrick, although the number of military personnel fell to half the wartime high of 2,300.[6] Research and development operations remained under control of a civilian director. By 1950, partly in response to the Korean War, the base's activities began to expand again. In 1956, Camp Detrick was designated Fort Detrick to symbolize the permanence of the facility.

Research at Detrick, according to its promotional literature, provided civilian as well as military benefits. But among the most ubiquitous of Detrick's contributions to civilian life is the herbicide 2,4,5–T, which contains dioxin.[7] Not mentioned in the promotional literature is the fact that dioxin is a nearly indestructible pollutant, lethal to a variety of animals and a threat to human health. No doubt it was developed to enhance the nation's security; few could have foreseen that later it would be found in waste dumps and other locations across the country. Large amounts have lain about for decades, belatedly recognized by local residents or health officials. Frequently no one knows where it came from.

In the postwar years Fort Detrick shared research projects with the

Public Health Service, the Department of Agriculture, and the Army Medical Corps.[8] By the late 1960s the base had become the largest employer in Frederick County; its public relations office emphasized not only the number of jobs it provided in the community but the benefit of its research to "public welfare, health, and safety."[9]

The official history published in 1968 reveals little about the base's "primary mission," work on biological warfare, "because of military security."[10] The only hint about the open air tests over populated areas appeared in an oblique reference under a paragraph headed "Experimental Airborne Infection." After mentioning that procedures had been developed to assess "microbial aerosols and experimentally induced infections," the paragraph concludes with the cryptic comment that "novel approaches are being applied to evaluate the role of the airborne route of transmission in the naturally acquired respiratory diseases that play such an important role in both civilian and military public health."[11] Not until a decade later would citizens learn that the "novel approaches" included secretly spraying the public with bacteria and chemicals.

In 1969, when President Nixon announced the end of the United States' offensive biological warfare program, a large facility was already under construction at Detrick to house medical research associated with biological warfare. The sprawling structure was completed in 1971 and became the home of the U.S. Army Medical Research Institute of Infectious Diseases (USAMRIID). It has become the principal location on the base for continued biological warfare research. Costing $18 million, the building sits on the edge of a complex of older facilities, some of which are still part of the biological warfare program, others having been converted to cancer research facilities.

Current Biological Warfare Research

In 1983 the army issued a 16-page brochure that described current activities at Fort Detrick. The brochure begins with the statement that "there is no longer any mystery about Fort Detrick," a view that was questioned during conversations with a dozen local residents. The base and its personnel, the brochure states, are presently "as important to the National Defense as the soldiers who man weapons at the world's outposts." This contention remains unamplified, as does the booklet's claim that Fort Detrick is "the Free World's leading microbiological containment research campus."[12] Such statements, as will be shown, have done little to allay the concerns of skeptics.

The 1983 brochure devotes two pages to discussion of the research

being conducted at USAMRIID. It indicates that studies are underway involving "some of the most virulent and pathogenic microorganisms which are threats to U.S. military forces." The program includes study of a large array of viruses, bacteria, mycotoxins, and
marine toxins. A variety of diseases and agents that "possess significant BW potential" are under investigation, including the Lassa fever
virus, Ebola virus, various hemorrhagic fever viruses, botulism and
anthrax toxins, T-2 and other mycotoxins, equine encephalomyelitis,
Q fever, tularemia, yellow fever, and Rift Valley fever. The list is
imposing and the toxins and diseases formidable, yet the reader is
assured that "there is no risk to the surrounding community."[13]

While providing this assurance, the booklet fails to mention some
unsettling facts. Beside the questionable statement that there is no
longer mystery about activities at the base, the brochure contains no
mention of "hot spots" that remain contaminated and off-limits. And
while the brochure implies that none of the present work is secret,
visitors may not enter certain sections within the USAMRIID facility
or other locations on the base. Moreover, the army's booklet offers no
hint that extensive genetic engineering is now being carried out in the
biological warfare laboratories. In 1980 USAMRIID advertised for
scientists to offer proposals on the introduction of human nervous
system genes into bacteria through recombinant DNA methods.[14]
The army sought and received special permission from the National
Institutes of Health to perform recombinant DNA experiments that
involve cloning toxigenic genes into *Escherichia coli,* bacteria commonly found in the human intestine.[15]

Detrick's Believers

Norman Covert looks younger than the forty years he admits to. He is
an engaging spokesman for Fort Detrick and seems well suited to be
head of its public affairs office. He has held the position since 1977,
and one of his tasks is to convince people that secret work is no longer
taking place at the base. "We keep being asked that question, and we
keep saying no, we are not developing biological weapons. We are not
doing any offensive studies."[16]

Covert reviews for a visitor the kind of work the base is involved
with as part of the defensive biological warfare program. He speaks
with pride of the 450 scientists and supporting staff who are "studying
traditional biological agents—all the ones that have been used in the
past." He insists that no new agents—through recombinant DNA or
other means—are being developed. Protection against known agents,

like those that cause hemorrhagic diseases, has been difficult enough to deal with, and "many of them are still stymieing the group."

Covert is not happy about the nation's present defensive capabilities. He asks rhetorically, "Is America ready if we were attacked using biological weapons?" and answers, "I don't think so. That seems to be the consensus because we don't know what it will be, how it will be delivered." Why then, an outsider asks, limit investigation to traditional agents? Do not recombinant DNA techniques offer the possibility of creating new organisms that would be even harder to develop defenses against? Covert does not yield. "As the scientists tell me, recombinant DNA is an awful lot of trouble to go through to develop a biological weapon. We could do it in the basement with standard techniques and come up with an effective weapon."

Around the time that Covert made this statement, Professors Susan Wright, a historian of science at the University of Michigan, and Robert Sinsheimer, a biophysicist and chancellor at the University of California at Santa Cruz, cited fourteen recombinant DNA research projects being sponsored by the Department of Defense. While none appeared designed to produce biological weapons, "the kinds and extent of the Department's biological research—particularly the types contemplated as a response to threat of enemy use of genetic manipulation techniques—may raise doubts that such work will or can be completely in accord with the spirit" of the Biological Weapons Convention.[17] Little more than a year later, an advertisement in *Science* magazine requested proposals for recombinant DNA studies involving enterotoxin bacteria, for immunization and diagnosis studies. The sponsoring authority was at Fort Detrick.[18]

None of this means that the army is violating treaty commitments. Yet Covert's dismissal of gene splicing as a technique to make weapons leaves one wondering why the army uses the technique to develop protection against weapons. The inconsistency remains unanswered.

In discussion about vulnerability testing, Covert dismisses the possibility that the germs sprayed in populated areas caused harm. The one that was implicated in infection and death during the spraying of San Francisco, *Serratia marcescens,* "was a harmless bacteria," he says, "and at this time we still believe that. There has been nothing to the contrary, nothing concrete."

When asked about the army's reserving the right to continue such tests, Covert responds, "I would say that we want to retain that," and cites Fort Detrick's help in solving the Legionnaire's Disease mystery. An outbreak of an apparently unknown disease during an American Legion convention at a Philadelphia hotel in 1976 killed twenty-nine people. Public health officials searched in vain for the cause. They called Fort Detrick, Covert says, because "we have an extensive aerobiology capability, which means we can test the flow of organisms through the air. Our people agreed to help because it could very well have been a biological warfare attack." He said the Fort Detrick staff showed that the unidentified organism was thriving in the water of the hotel's air conditioning system, "and then being sent right back out into the hotel air ducts." Not until a year later was the organism identified.

The listener wonders how any of this helped in the context of biological warfare and developing defenses. Covert is asked, could not the outbreak still have been produced by an enemy attack? "It could have been. It could have been. So I would say they were smart in reserving the right to conduct such vulnerability tests." He trails his response with a pronouncement: "Always leave that option open to us."

Would resumed testing be like the earlier tests in cities and in subways, and would it be conducted again in secret? Covert answers indirectly. "They would have to find an area. I don't believe they would do it in the New York subways again—they would have to find another area. But I don't think there is any question that we have vulnerabilities." He continues, "It may be that they could duplicate a situation which does not put anyone in any potential peril, or anything that would raise questions about what they were doing."

The "they" Covert refers to are the scientists in the biological warfare program. He sees these people as talented and patriotic, but he implicitly suggests that ethical considerations are not their highest priorities. "We have a lot of smart people here, and I'm very proud of them all. I have seen them at work and I am very impressed with what they do, and their dedication. They are dedicated to science, not politics. So they stay out of that other game. You know, let somebody else fight that game. Let the commander of the institute go down to Congress and testify about what's going on. They don't want any part of it—'Just leave me to my laboratory and my work, and I'll produce for you.' And they're doing their work."

One of these scientists agreed to an interview on condition of anonymity. A civilian microbiologist, he was at Fort Detrick in the early 1950s, later worked for the army at other locations, and has been a senior administrator at Detrick since the 1970s. He recalls his excitement about working in the program before the United States renounced its larger effort. "We were morally right," he says, to try "to determine whether or not we could actually defend ourselves." He believes that biological weapons are unfairly cast as repugnant. "Having seen all kinds of war and warfare, I would much rather be exposed to this type of warfare than to some of the things we have today." In this he joins earlier enthusiasts who argued that biological weapons, unlike most others, could be used to debilitate and not kill, and would "cause no material damage."[19]

When asked about the vulnerability tests of the past, the scientist insists they had been fully justified. "We weren't trying to put something over on the public. . . . This was a scientific experiment. We didn't want any changes or modifications because we were doing this. In other words, if we told the public, maybe that would have closed off the public's coming and going. Now this would have changed the whole character of the experiment." Would the scientist use the same justification for simulated secret biological attacks today? "Yes, that's right."

The scientist couples his interest in preserving the "character of the experiment" with concern that the Soviets not gain information: "We felt that the less we informed the public, the less the Russians knew." He worries a great deal about the Soviet Union. "We're dealing with a clever group over there. Look what's going on in South America and Central America. Look at your map from 1940 to today and see how many countries have turned pink or red. That is spreading a lot faster than I am comfortable with."

When asked about the ethics of spraying people without their knowledge or consent, the scientist says he has thought about the issue many times. "But I also look at it remembering that a lot of people were destroyed in World War II before we woke up and did anything. . . . Our job is to protect the country."

Like Norman Covert, the Fort Detrick scientist-administrator maintains that the tests are harmless, that the bacterial agents were nontoxic. "If you or I were in the area in which the testing was being performed, we would have been far more at risk by having some bus partner or commuter partner walking down the hallway with us coughing and passing off tuberculosis germs, whooping cough organisms, pneumonia."

During a stroll around the base the scientist points wistfully at some of the low-flung wooden buildings. Now used for cancer research or other nonoffensive work, until 1969 each had been devoted to investigating and developing a particular biological warfare agent. A nearby structure contained the laboratories for organisms that cause tularemia, another for Q fever, a third for pneumonic plague. "The worst thing that Richard Nixon did was not his taping of conversations or lying about Watergate," says the Fort Detrick scientist." "The worst thing he did was to close down [some of] the biological warfare laboratories."

Neighborhood Skeptics

Not many neighbors share the scientist's nostalgia, and several continue to express discomfort about the base today. Suspicions have prompted some to believe that "Fort Detrick is more underground than above ground, and there aren't many people who are privy to exactly what is going on there." Mrs. Winnie Mulford, who made these comments, has lived in Frederick for seventeen years. She says she just does not like to think about the base. "I stay away from Fort Detrick—I have nothing to do with it." Her attitude is common among neighbors—outwardly unconcerned, but uncertain about what is happening inside the base.

Ann Weatherholt, a priest at All Saints Episcopal Church in Frederick, has worked with neighbors who have been involved in a variety of social issues, most recently those supporting a nuclear freeze. "But biological warfare has been pretty much a dead issue in recent years," she says. Perhaps someone could act as a catalyst and revive interest, she thinks, but that would not be easy. First, Frederick is a small, conservative town and most people don't like to "ruffle feathers." Then, "there is a philosophy among many people in this town that you don't bite the hand that feeds you, and Detrick is such a large employer."

Robert Hanson, a high school teacher in Frederick, thinks the community does not openly question activities at the base because "most of the people have always accepted Detrick in a patriotic way, as well as a source of jobs." Many simply assume that the government is doing the correct thing. A contrary perspective is offered by Wally Landes, who has been pastor of the Bush Creek Church of the Brethren for five years. He is convinced, because of conversations he has had with people who work there, that a vigorous biological warfare program is in progress at Detrick. He mentions a scientist who told him about his current work at the base involving counterattack capabilities.

Even if the research is for defensive purposes, Reverend Landes believes, "the public is being duped by labeling Detrick a cancer research center." He emphasizes that "they are continuing to create the kinds of organisms or agents that they were doing in the '50s and '60s." Calling the base a cancer research center "is a public relations cover-up to convince the public that the army is doing humane and benevolent experimentation." Landes concludes that if people knew what was really going on at the base, there would be active public opposition.

Landes's notion is based on two questionable assumptions. First, while suspicion about biological warfare activities at Detrick is common, it is based on speculation. Lacking evidence, one cannot be sure that Landes's views are valid. Second, even if harder evidence existed, an informed public still might not react. The jobs that Detrick provides and the conservative orientation of the community, as some residents point out, lessen the likelihood of public dissent. This was demonstrated in the 1960s when the United States was openly committed to a major biological warfare program. Despite common knowledge about Detrick's activities, a protest demonstration outside the base in the early 1960s attracted only a few hundred people.

Although spokesmen for Fort Detrick contend that the base's biological warfare program is defensive, modest, and medical in nature, even scientists who work on the base are not sure. Dr. Michael Yarmolinsky is a microbiologist who left the National Institutes of Health in 1976 to work in the cancer laboratories at Detrick. The cancer laboratories are associated with the National Cancer Institute and are entirely separate from the army's biological warfare laboratories. Yarmolinsky has long opposed any biological warfare programs, even refusing to visit the base in the past for this reason. He had been invited with other scientists in 1968 to celebrate Detrick's twenty-fifth anniversary—its silver jubilee. "I declined because I saw no reason for jubilation about what had been done here."

Does Dr. Yarmolinsky think that activities are now being conducted beyond those officially acknowledged? "My own feeling is that I honestly don't know," he says. "I would be very appreciative if someone could find out. There have been advertisements in science magazines for molecular biologists interested in cloning work at Fort Detrick. So presumably this might involve the cloning of toxins and that sort of thing. Some of this could be useful work, although one wonders always what the motivation is."

The Tower, the building contaminated with anthrax spores, evokes little concern. In contrast to the locals near Gruinard Island, none of Fort Detrick's neighbors seems to worry about an accidental release of the bacteria. The mood is reflected in the comments by Weatherholt, Yarmolinsky, and Hanson. None is a supporter of the biological warfare program, and all are aware of the potential hazard presented by the Tower. Yet none showed much concern when asked about it.

Weatherholt: "I know that the building exists and that it is contaminated with anthrax, but that's about all I know. I think people know, but they kind of forget about it. Their lives are involved in other things, and I think they just feel that it's behind the fence at Detrick and is 'their' problem, not 'mine.' I haven't seen any reaction from anyone on the subject. I guess I know it exists more from local lore than anything else."

Yarmolinsky: "I am within sight of the Tower most of the time. I look at it this way: There are pigeons roosting on that building, and if one day I walk along and see a dead pigeon I may react. But I really don't know now what can be done. Certainly people are aware of the extraordinary danger that the disease presents. I don't like the idea of the building eventually crumbling, and nobody presumably doing anything about it. But I guess there are many such hazards in the world, and one comes to accept them as long as nothing seems to be happening."

Hanson: "I guess the people I have talked to about [the Tower] who work in Fort Detrick feel secure about it. They do not indicate that it's a matter of the wind blowing the door open and anthrax being spread over Frederick County. But I do understand the problem will last indefinitely. . . . I have seen people just shrug their shoulders and accept it because they say it's a technology they can't understand. Then I have seen the opposite—people say, 'I'm moving out of this area because we have such a high incidence of these kind of diseases. We're downwind from Detrick and I'm sure there is something going on that they don't tell us about. So I can't stand it, and I'm going to move.'

"I have had several such conversations," Hanson continues, "and do know of people who moved for this reason. But that's the minority view. The majority view is more one of quiet skepticism—'we just don't know what's going on in there, but nothing bad has happened yet.' It's all very hush-hush. I don't feel like I ever get to the bottom of it."

These attitudes are typical among neighbors of the base. While assurances about the safety and limitations of America's biological warfare program are not openly contested, uncertainty lies beneath the surface. Unlike in Scotland, even the most avid skeptics appear unwilling to mount public challenges. The larger questions simply go unaddressed: What are the roots of the colossal misjudgments that produced legacies of potential disease and danger in the Tower and other "hot spots"? Can these problems be rectified? How can the public be protected from similar problems that might arise from present and future biological warfare programs?

Notes

1. Richard M. Clendenin, *Science and Technology at Fort Detrick, 1943–1968* (Frederick, Md.: Fort Detrick, Historian, Technical Information Division, April 1968), pp. x–xi.

2. Ibid., p. 10.

3. Ibid., pp. 10–12.

4. Ibid., p. 7.

5. U.S. Congress: Senate Hearings before the Subcommittee on Health and Scientific Research of the Committee on Human Resources, *Biological Testing Involving Human Subjects by the Department of Defense,* 1977, March 8 and May 23, 1977 (Washington, D. C.: Government Printing Office, 1977), p. 68.

6. Clendenin, *Science and Technology at Fort Detrick,* p. 26.

7. Ibid., p. 46; Seymour M. Hersh, *Chemical and Biological Warfare: America's Hidden Arsenal* (Indianapolis: Bobbs-Merrill, 1968), p. 99.

8. Clendenin, *Science and Technology,* pp. 31–34.

9. Ibid., pp. 38–44.

10. Ibid., pp. 44–46.

11. Ibid., p. 44.

12. *Fort Detrick,* U.S. Army, Health Services Command (n.d.), p. 1. (The public affairs office at Fort Detrick indicated publication was in 1983.)

13. Ibid., pp. 6–7.

14. *Science* 209, no. 4462 (September 12, 1980): 1282.

15. *Environment* 24, no. 6 (July/August 1982): 4.

16. Interviews with Fort Detrick officials and neighboring residents cited in this chapter were conducted by telephone and visits to the base in 1983 and 1984.

17. Susan Wright and Robert Sinsheimer, "Recombinant DNA and Biological Warfare," *Bulletin of the Atomic Scientists* 39, no. 9 (November 1983): 23.

18. *Science* 227, no. 4686 (February 1, 1985): 468.

19. J. H. Rothschild, Brigadier General, U.S.A. (Ret.), *Tomorrow's Weapons, Chemical and Biological* (New York: McGraw-Hill, 1964), p. 21.

5

The Army's Germ Warfare Simulants
How Dangerous Are They?

SENATOR SCHWEIKER: I think what concerns me more is that I believe supposedly there should have been some sort of monitoring system set up. I guess my question is . . . did in fact the people responsible for these tests establish a monitoring system to check on whether pneumonia-like illnesses occurred in these areas such as this, where the rate tripled in the test year, compared to years before and years after the test?

GENERAL AUGERSON: As far as I know, Senator, I am not aware of any special surveillance system established to monitor the changes in the incident of various conditions in surrounding communities as part of that program.[1]

PERHAPS THE MOST IMPORTANT question about the army's open air testing program concerns the danger of the simulant agents involved. The army has repeatedly contended that none of the millions of people who have been exposed during the tests has suffered ill effects. In a memorandum to Congress in 1977, the army sought to assure everyone by insisting that it used only biological warfare simulants "considered by the scientific community to be totally safe."[2] The official position was that the simulant agents were harmless and, by implication, that there was nothing wrong with using them in the past and nothing wrong with using them now.

There are several difficulties with this position. By the army's admission, the health of the exposed populations was never monitored during or after any of the earlier tests. Yet when challenged with data that suggest the germs had caused disease, army spokesmen invariably denied the possibility. How could they know if there was no monitoring? Another problem arises from the army's own characterizations of the simulants it used. Material the army submitted to the Senate subcommittee hearings in 1977 on the biological warfare tests acknowledged that some of the agents may not have been entirely

44

innocuous. The recognition was tentative and qualified, but it stood in contradiction to the official line that the program was totally safe.

In addition, the army has never explained its apparent obliviousness during the time of the tests to the scientific literature that indicated that the simulants could be harmful. Finally, testimony by respected scientists has held that any microorganism under certain conditions may be dangerous to humans, and many scientists have therefore condemned the spraying of any kind of biological warfare simulants as dangerous to segments of the population. Yet the army's position remains that it will conduct open air tests whenever it thinks necessary. A review of the four simulants most commonly used questions the wisdom of this position.

Aspergillus Fumigatus

Aspergillus fumigatus is a fungus that the army used during tests in the 1950s over populated areas. In a report provided during the Senate hearings in 1977, the army suggested that the organism posed little danger to humans. It conceded that the organism "is considered an opportunist causing aspergillosis in debilitated persons," but contended that *Aspergillus fumigatus* is unremarkable and implied that there was nothing wrong with spraying it because the organism is all around us anyway: "It is ubiquitous in nature and can be cultured from soil, water, air, food stuffs, animal waste products and most human body orifices."[3]

The report is misleading in two respects. First, in saying that the army stopped using aspergillus after the 1950s, though not explaining why, there is an inference that until then the army might not have realized the organism could be "considered" harmful. Second, as the army would have it, only debilitated persons are at risk. Both of these propositions are wrong.

Aspergillus fumigatus has long been known to cause aspergillosis, a disease not merely "considered" to affect debilitated people, but one to which any person may fall victim. Standard medical reference works before and during the testing program make this clear. A textbook published in 1951 noted that the danger of aspergillus had been recognized since the nineteenth century.[4] A description of the organism published in 1949 indicates that *Aspergillus fumigatus* is "important as a contaminant of lesions and as an agent of infection." A cause of aspergillosis, it could lead to "infections of lungs, bronchi, external ear, paranasal sinuses, orbit, bones, and meninges."[5]

The organism was known to cause death, and not just in previously debilitated persons. Although some types of infections caused by aspergillus were not especially threatening, this was not true "for the pulmonary and generalized infections, which frequently are fatal," according to a sourcebook on medical diagnosis and therapy.[6] Since the army tests involved inhalation of aspergillus spores, the risk was of a pulmonary nature.

Portions of a report about an army test in 1951 involving *Aspergillus fumigatus* were released in 1980 in response to a Freedom of Information Act request. They indicate that the army intentionally exposed a disproportionate number of black people to the organism. The testers imagined that an enemy might use a more lethal fungus that affects blacks in particular, and that assessing the dispersal of aspergillus among these people would help prepare defenses against an attack. Thus in 1951 at the Norfolk Supply Center in Virginia, unsuspecting workers were handling crates that had been contaminated by the army with aspergillus spores. From the report: "Within this [Naval Supply System] there are employed large numbers of laborers, including many Negroes, whose incapacities would seriously affect the operation of the supply system. Since Negroes are more susceptible to coccidioides than are whites, this fungus disease was simulated by using Aspergillus fumigatus Mutant C-2."[7]

Disclosure in 1980 of the racial aspect of the experiment did little to lessen skepticism about the army's interest in the public's welfare. At the same time, Pentagon spokesmen were insisting that "the Norfolk experiment had resulted in no illnesses or other adverse health effects."[8] The army provided no evidence to support this contention. It had admitted at the 1977 Senate hearings that no one monitored people's health during any of the tests. Yet now, twenty-nine years after the Norfolk test, it was claiming that no one was affected.

Zinc Cadmium Sulfide

In 1980, around the time that the public learned about the Norfolk test involving aspergillus, another army report revealed that a chemical agent called zinc cadmium sulfide was widely used in the germ warfare tests. The agent is a dry fluorescent powder that has been sprayed sometimes in the company of biological agents, sometimes by itself. The rationale for using the chemical is that detection devices could easily identify dispersion patterns of fluorescent material.

The army's 1977 list of 239 acknowledged biological warfare tests mentions that zinc cadmium sulfide had been used in 34. Evidence later made public indicates that the chemical had been sprayed over areas not mentioned in the 1977 list, including parts of Iowa, Nebraska, South Dakota, and Virginia.[9] Thus the number of biological warfare tests in populated areas exceeds the figure supplied by the army—by how much, we do not know.

Despite its frequent use, zinc cadmium sulfide's safety during field tests was never established. In a 1965 article by scientists who had helped develop the chemical for the army's use, the scientist-authors reviewed the validity of its use as an atmospheric tracer and listed several criteria that any tracer should meet. These criteria included detectability in small amounts, the availability of convenient measuring devices, low cost, control over rate of dispersion, and stability in the atmosphere. The last item on the list was the suggestion that the material not be toxic.[10] While the authors discuss in detail most of the listed criteria in relationship to zinc cadmium sulfide, the question of toxicity is not mentioned again. Evidently the testers simply assumed that the chemical was harmless.

Shortly afterward, a paper by L. Arthur Spomer indicated that zinc cadmium sulfide in the quantities sprayed by the army was indeed toxic to humans. Spomer, a professor in the School of Agriculture at the University of Illinois, had worked in the biological warfare program and knew about the army's use of the chemical as a simulant. He showed that the cadmium component, in particular, was long known to be dangerous. To sustain his claim he cited a number of studies, fifteen of which had been published before or during the testing program, some as early as 1932. When introduced into humans, cadmium accumulates in tissues and "is known to be toxic to almost all physiological systems."[11]

Spomer summarized his concerns, referring to cadmium as Cd and to zinc cadmium sulfide as FP (fluorescent particles):

> Although Cd toxicity is well-established and FP is commonly used as a tracer in atmospheric studies, no case of Cd poisoning resulting from the use of FP has been reported in the literature. This may be because none has occurred; however, it is more likely that such poisoning has been of a low-level chronic nature and its symptoms are less dramatic and more difficult to recognize than in the case of acute Cd poisoning. A general ignorance of the toxicity of FP and of the symptoms of Cd poisoning also contribute to the failure to recognize FP poisoning.[12]

In 1980, after public disclosure that the army had sprayed zinc cadmium sulfide for at least two decades in populated areas, and in response to an inquiry about its toxicity, a Pentagon spokesman declared that the chemical was entirely harmless. Said Major Lee

DeLorme on behalf of the army, "Ingesting zinc cadmium sulfide is like swallowing a pebble. It is a nonsoluble material. It would pass through you."[13]

Bacillus Subtilis

Bacillus subtilis has been one of the two bacteria most commonly used during simulated biological warfare attacks. It is referred to in various army reports as *Bacillus globigii* (BG) or *Bacillus subtilis variant niger*, but it is the same organism. The designation "niger" (black) describes the particular strain that the army deployed.[14]

The army used Bacillus subtilis because the germ shares characteristics with bacteria like *Bacillus anthracis*, a biological warfare agent that causes anthrax. Both bacteria may exist in spore form, a condition in which they take on a natural armor-like coat. When in contact with a warm, moist environment, like the lungs or an open wound, they transform into a vegetative and active stage. Spores can exist for extraordinarily long periods, in effect waiting for an environment conducive to their active stage.

Arthur Rose, author of a text on chemical microbiology, has characterized a spore as a "highly efficient survival pack, because it is as much as 10,000 times as resistant to heat as the vegetative cell, and up to 100 times more resistant to ultraviolet radiation. It can survive for years, possibly centuries, in the absence of nutrients."[15] (These characteristics are the basis of the virtually permanent infection with anthrax spores of Gruinard Island and parts of Fort Detrick.)

The army's 1977 report contends that the *Bacillus subtilis* used in its tests "was and is still considered by medical authorities to be harmless (nonpathogenic) to man." It states further that a search of the literature indicated that "there is no evidence of infection in man or experimental animals following exposure to BG spores, even in massive doses."[16]

The statement is not true. A standard textbook on bacteriology documents that *Bacillus subtilis,* though considered harmless to most people, may cause infections and invade the "blood stream in cachetic [debilitating] diseases."[17] Another conventional reference book includes *Bacillus subtilis* in a group of bacteria that cause "infections in man; pulmonary and disseminated infections in immunologically compromised hosts; localized infections in a closed space (e.g., opthalmitis, meningitis); wound infections following trauma, surgery, or the introduction of foreign prosthetic material."[18]

Beyond the direct pathogenicity that has been associated with *Bacillus subtilis,* in the 1950s the organism was shown to have an unusually simple capability of genetic transformation. It readily could incorporate segments of infective viral material (DNA) into its own genetic structures. This led some scientists to suggest that the bacteria could act as reservoirs for pathogenic viruses and "serve as 'carriers' until some later time when the virus becomes active and causes the disease for no readily apparent reason."[19]

Thus, the army's claims about the innocence of *Bacillus subtilis* are inaccurate. There was evidence to the contrary in the literature during the 1950s and 1960s while the earlier tests were being conducted, and there was more evidence by the time the report was issued in 1977. In 1986, the army acknowledged that it was still making "extensive use" of these and other bacteria ("simulants") in open air "operational testing."[20] Its position is that the bacteria "was and is" harmless to human beings. Do all the scientists who have been involved with the tests believe this to be so?

Hints of skepticism appeared as early as 1961. A revealing paper was published then as part of the proceedings of an international symposium in Britain on *Inhaled Particles and Vapours*. The author was Dr. Carlton E. Brown of the U.S. Army Chemical Corps, Fort Detrick, Maryland, and his paper was titled "Human Retention from Single Inhalations of Bacillus Subtilis Spore Aerosols."[21] Brown's paper was based on an experiment involving the inhalation of *Bacillus subtilis* spores by a human subject. He elaborately described his apparatus and method, from the preparation of the aerosol through the counting of the inhaled spores. An excerpt describes the subject's role:

> 1. The subject placed the mouth- or nosepiece in position; 2. The mouth- or nosepiece was connected [to the apparatus containing the bacilli] as required; 3. The subject breathed several breaths of room air through the unconnected respiratory opening, or the respiratory opening connected to the sampler-intake line, to allow his respiration to return to "normal;" 4. The subject selected the time to inhale, in retention tests, or to exhale, in displacement tests; 5. In inhalations, the subject . . . opened the stopcock in the line to the aerosol chamber [and] inhaled.[22]

The tests were conducted in June 1959. Brown reports that as few as 100 spores and as many as 1,280 were taken in by the subject during a test, depending on the length of time and intensity of the inhalation. By measuring total spore exhalation, he determined that about 20 percent of the inhaled spores were retained by the subject.[23] He further describes in detail the estimated spore distribution in various parts of the subject's respiratory system during testing, using tables, figures, statistical analyses, and lengthy narrative. Only three lines are devoted to describing the subject. We are told that he was an adult male, given his height, weight, and lung capacity, and informed that his "respiratory system was normal according to medical and X-ray examinations."[24]

Nothing is said about possibly harmful effects of the tests, nor is there indication that the subject's health was monitored during or after his participation. If the subject's pre-test X-ray or medical examinations had indicated the presence of illness, one wonders whether he would have been considered suitable for the inhalation experiment. The secret spraying of *Bacillus subtilis* and other agents over populated areas had long been underway and would continue for years. Millions of subjects at all stages of life and in all manner of infirmity were being exposed. Moreover, exposed individuals were breathing not just hundreds of spores as in the Brown experiment, but millions.

Following Brown's presentation, several conference participants joined in discussion. The transcript of the proceedings indicates that most were involved with the biological warfare programs in the United States or Great Britain. Dr. J. Clifford Spendlove of the U.S. Army Chemical Corps asked Brown if the spores were washed in distilled water before they were dispersed. Dr. R. J. Shephard of the British Chemical Defense Establishment at Porton Down found particularly interesting Brown's findings about the effect of breath-holding on the number of spores retained by the subject. Professor T. H. Hatch of the University of Pittsburgh asked Brown if he had measured increases in the size of the spores once they entered a moist environment.[25]

These comments and questions typified the discussion, which dealt exclusively with the mechanics of the experiment. Toward the end of the session, Brown made a remarkable statement: "I would like to say I am a little surprised that no-one asked who inhaled these spores, and were there any particular problems involved in such experiments."[26] The issue was evidently not one that scientists at the conference had thought about. Brown quickly sought to defuse any concerns that he might have prompted by assuring the group that there were no problems. Yet his explanation ends with a curious confession that not everyone who knew about the experiment at Fort Detrick agreed: "When I went to our Safety Department and asked the doctor about such inhalations, he said I probably breathed worse than that every day. The only question was from our bacteriologist, who tried to discourage me with gruesome stories."[27]

Several scientists in the audience apparently became self-conscious after Brown called attention to their neglect. They inquired obliquely about the effects of the bacteria and the number left inside the subject. One asked, "What happened to these spores after they were inhaled and after retention? Did your bacteriological friends tell you?" From a second: "What about viability of the organism? Can you guarantee 100 percent recovery of the spores?" And another: "You were not able to do a control experiment, collecting the spores on a precipitator and comparing the direct spore count with the count after cultivation?" Brown's answer to the last question, as to the others, was scarcely informative. "This has been done, but not this time." With these cryptic words the session ended.

The issues that Brown raised, some of them inadvertently, point to contradictions in the army's official position. Although Brown says that safety was a consideration when planning the experiment, he reports only two professional opinions in this regard. A doctor told him the experiment would be safe, while a bacteriologist disagreed. Despite the skepticism, not only was the experiment conducted, but there is no indication that the health of the subject was monitored.

This approach has been consistent with the army's large-scale experiments involving unwitting populations. In the case of the field tests, however, the subjects include old and debilitated people, and the number of inhaled organisms are thousands of times greater than in Brown's experiment.

No less instructive was the response of the scientists to Brown's paper. None voiced interest in the safety of the human subject until Brown raised the matter, and even then their questions were hardly challenging. More to the point would have been questions about monitoring the subject's health during and after the test, what the subject had been told concerning the safety of the experiment, what specifically the bacteriologist had warned against, and whether the experiment could be justified ethically in view of the known infective potential of *Bacillus subtilis*.

Why Brown raised the issue of safety, and then cited the bacteriologist's skepticism, is unclear. But in doing so he and the scientists he addressed tell us more than the army's official disclaimers would have us believe. If there were doubts expressed by a scientist about the safety of this lone experiment, there surely must have been doubts about the more expansive tests over populated areas. Yet even when the safety issue was raised at the symposium, the scientists who asked questions revealed little serious concern.

The participants at the conference, like others engaged in biological warfare experimentation, did not appear invidious or sadistic. They assumed there was no danger because they wanted to believe there was none. Any suggestive evidence to the contrary was ignored, as were the few scientists who expressed skepticism. The vast majority conformed with the accepted belief system and behaved as most people do. It has always been easier to comply and acquiesce than to object and stand out.

Bacillus subtilis is still considered by the army to be harmless. That is why the army has no compunction about calling it a realistic "nontoxic" simulant that can be used in field tests over populated areas.

Serratia Marcescens

Beside *Bacillus subtilis,* the most commonly used organism in the army tests has been *Serratia marcescens,* whose use has evoked far more controversy than any other testing agent. Questions about its safety became a central issue during a federal court trial in 1981. The U.S. government was charged with responsibility for the death of a citizen as a consequence of a germ warfare test over San Francisco thirty years earlier. Some of the testimony about the serratia released in the test bears on this discussion.

Serratia marcescens has been used as a tracer because it produces a red pigment that makes it readily identifiable. Although the bacteria had been assumed by many to be relatively harmless, its safety was called into question early in the testing program. The army sprayed the San Francisco Bay area with serratia in September 1950. Four days later a patient at the Stanford University hospital was found to be suffering from an infection caused by *Serratia marcescens,* the first such case ever recorded at the hospital. During the following five months ten more patients at the hospital became infected by the bacteria, one of whom died as a result.

Doctors at the hospital were baffled. They knew nothing about the army's tests, and the outbreak was so extraordinary that members of the department of medicine wrote an article about it that appeared the following year in the American Medical Association's *Archives of Internal Medicine.* The article indicates that although the bacteria had been "considered essentially nonpathogenic in man," a search of the literature found "scattered reports describing the potential pathogenic properties of the organisms."[28]

The army had learned about the epidemic of serratia infections at the hospital, and secretly convened a committee of four scientists to assess the situation. The scientists concluded that the outbreak of serratia infections "appeared coincidental." They recommended that the use of *Serratia marcescens* "as a simulant should be continued, even over populated areas, when such studies are necessary for the advancement of the biological warfare program."[29]

During the next two decades the army continued to spray huge amounts of serratia and other bacterial and chemical agents over populated areas across the United States. Increasing numbers of serratia infections were reported, and by the end of the 1970s the bacteria had become recognized "as a cause of serious infection in man."[30]

In a comprehensive article about *Serratia marcescens* published in 1979, Victor Yu, a specialist in infectious diseases, reviewed the changed perspectives of the medical community toward the organism. He reaffirms that although serratia was known to have caused infections in animals and man before the 1950s, it was considered to be generally harmless. But during the 1950s and 1960s increasing numbers of reports suggested that its pathogenicity had been underrated. Yu cites a study in the early 1950s that documented the organism's responsibility for cases of meningitis, wound infection, and arthritis. He mentions another that described *Serratia marcescens* as the source of a nursery epidemic involving 27 babies. Additional studies reported the transmission of serratia infections during common hospital procedures such as dialysis, blood transfusions, catheterization, and lumbar puncture.[31] Yu lists 106 articles among his references, almost all of which indicate the pathogenicity of *Serratia marcescens*. Sixty-three of the articles appeared before 1970, the period during which the army acknowledges spraying the organisms around the country.

Some medical analysts have linked the army tests to the increased incidence of serratia infections. In 1976 John Mills, a professor at the University of California Medical Center in San Francisco, found that *Serratia marcescens* infections in the San Francisco Bay area had increased dramatically since the 1960s. The rate had become five to ten times greater than at other locations, he estimated. He wondered if the earlier tests "could have seeded the Bay area environment" with the germs.[32] A spokesman for the army, Colonel Ignacio Hernandez-Fragoso, denied the possibility of any relationship. "The likelihood of those [organisms] perpetuating to this day," said the colonel in 1977, "is nil."[33] But Lawrence K. Altman, a physician and medical writer for the *New York Times*, wrote: "So little is known about the phenomenon, and the biological aspects of the situation are so complex, that it appears virtually impossible to make a scientific judgment about whether the biological warfare tests caused the hospital cases."[34]

The army contends that none of its previous tests, including those involving *Serratia marcescens*, created any problems. The official position is that all the army's test agents were harmless simulants of lethal germs and, as affirmed in its 1977 report to Congress, all "activities in the BW program were conducted under the safest and most controlled conditions possible."[35] A senior scientist at the army's biological warfare headquarters in Fort Detrick reconfirmed this view to me during an interview in 1983. When asked specifically about *Serratia marcescens,* he contended that the organism "is really harmless." The army continues to use serratia as a "simulant" of "toxic airborne biological materials."[36]

The Notion of Safe Simulants

"There is no such thing as a microorganism that cannot cause trouble," testified George H. Connell in 1977 during the Senate hearings on biological warfare testing. Connell, the assistant to the director of the Centers for Disease Control, continued, "If you get the right concentration at the right place, at the right time, and in the right person, something is going to happen."[37]

In a sense, this recognition renders superfluous our review of the dangers associated with the agents used in the field tests. Even noting that the army ignored evidence that its simulants may have been causing disease misses a larger point. By considering only the agents that were used, one might assume that other simulants would be suitable. If Connell is correct, no agent is suitable.

Microbiologists have long understood that bacteria considered to be innocuous in one situation will not necessarily remain so under other conditions. Increasing the numbers of bacteria and exposing them to humans for lengthy periods could alter their ability to affect the health of the exposed population. This is true for any bacteria. No biological warfare simulant, accordingly, can truly be considered safe. Thus with the knowledge that the army may be continuing open air testing, one returns to questions raised by Senator Edward Kennedy at the 1977 Senate hearings: "Is it safe? Are we sure? Do scientists agree?"[38]

Only the last question can be answered unequivocally. Scientists do not agree. Despite the army's view that the program is safe, sharply critical testimony was offered at the hearings. Connell's comments were echoed by others like Matthew Meselson, chairman of the Department of Biochemistry and Molecular Biology at Harvard University: "Often our knowledge of the disease potential of an organism is based on cases in which the aerosol route is not the primary route, and that leads us to have confidence that some organisms are not very hazardous. However, the situation can be quite different if the organism is in aerosol form." Meselson, like Connell, testified that "any organism dispersed as an aerosol over a human population can lead to trouble."[39]

Two other scientists who testified at the hearings introduced comprehensive written statements. The statements are unforgiving, as the following excerpts show. From Stephen Weitzman, a physician and microbiologist at the State University of New York, Stony Brook:

> Our understanding of a biological simulant, that is, a live bacteria that does not produce disease, is based on our past experience with that agent under *certain definite conditions* [original italics]. If these conditions change, the bacteria can cause disease. There are at least two components to these conditions: One is the number of bacteria and the second is the state of health of the people exposed. . . . In summary, too many uncontrolled variables are present to consider vulnerability testing safe, of large civilian populations with a biological simulant.[40]

Dr. J. M. Joseph, director of laboratories administration for the Maryland State Department of Health and Mental Hygiene, expressed particular concern about the use of *Serratia marcescens.* He noted that serratia infections had been described in the literature since 1913, and increasingly so during the time of the army tests. He deplored the army's apparent inattention to these reports: "Since it was known that a clear danger of Serratia marcescens infection existed for hospitalized and debilitated individuals, it is inconceivable and unconscionable that the organism would have been spread as an aerosol over unsuspecting masses of people, some of whom would have been at high risk." Joseph completed his statement with an emphatic condemnation: "Mass environmental exposure on the scale conducted by the Army was apparently unnecessary on its scientific merit and constituted an unjustifiable health hazard for a particular segment of the population. To rationalize the validity for the study would be sheer folly."[41]

In 1984, on contract from the army, a committee of the Board on Army Science and Technology of the National Academy of Sciences concluded that the need for further open air testing was "critical." It urged the use of "realistic, nontoxic simulants" in such tests—precisely the kind of simulants the army claims it has been using all along.[42]

Conclusion

None of the four agents that the army admits using over populated areas in simulated biological warfare attacks is harmless. Reports in the open scientific literature before and during the time of the tests raised questions about the safety of each biological and chemical agent. Moreover, accepted biological principles, then as now, should have precluded the large-scale use of any simulants in field tests involving human targets. How then may the testing be accounted for? Are testers venal and sadistic? Naive? Irrational? None of these adjectives seems appropriate.

Administrators of the past and present biological warfare programs are convinced that their work enhances the nation's security. A firm mind-set is evident during conversations with scientists and others who have worked on the program. Many believe that a chemical or biological attack from an enemy is likely, and that risks from their own "simulated" attacks are virtually nil.

Yet when exposing people to the simulated agents, the possibility of harmful effects, especially among compromised hosts like the very young, the very old, and the debilitated, is incontestable. The testers have ignored this fact at the expense of people's health and of their rights, as experimental subjects, to informed consent.

Notes

1. U.S. Congress: Senate Hearings before the Subcommittee on Health and Scientific Research of the Committee on Human Resources, *Biological Testing Involving Human Subjects by the Department of Defense, 1977*, March 8 and May 23, 1977 (Washington, D.C.: Government Printing Office, 1977), pp. 18–19.

2. "Information for Members of Congress: U.S. Army Activities in the U.S. Biological Warfare (BW) Program." Report furnished by the Chief of Legislative Liaison, Department of the Army, March 8, 1977, p. 4.

3. Senate Hearings, *Biological Testing*, p. 110.

4. Russell L. Cecil and Robert F. Loeb, eds., *Textbook of Medicine*, 8th ed. (Philadelphia: W. B. Saunders, 1951), p. 319.

5. Harold Wellington Jones, M.D., Norman L. Hoerr, M.D., and Arthur Osol, Ph.D., eds., *Blakiston's New Gould Medical Dictionary* (Philadelphia: The Blakiston Co., 1949), p. 101.

6. *The Merck Manual*, 10th ed. (Rahway, N.J.: Merck and Co., 1961), p. 939.

7. Quoted in News Release from the Office of Congressman G. William Whitehurst, 2nd District Virginia, September 17, 1980.

8. *Virginia-Pilot* (Norfolk, Va.), September 13, 1980, p. A-1; Robert Harris and Jeremy Paxman, *A Higher Form of Killing* (New York: Hill & Wang, 1982), pp. 156–57.

9. "U.S. Army Activity in the U.S. Biological Warfare Program," Vol. 1, February 1977, included in Senate Hearings, *Biological Testing*, pp. 125–40; *The Sun* (Baltimore), August 15, 1980; *Washington Post*, June 9, 1980, p. A-11.

10. Philip A. Leighton, William A. Perkins, Stuart W. Grinnel and Francis X. Webster, "The Fluorescent Particle Atmospheric Tracer," *Journal of Applied Meteorology* 4 (June 1965): 334.

11. L. Arthur Spomer, "Fluorescent Particle Atmospheric Tracer: Toxicity Hazard," *Atmospheric Environment* 7 (1973): 353.

12. Ibid.

13. *Chicago Tribune*, August 14, 1980.

14. "U.S. Army Activity," in Senate Hearings, *Biological Testing*, p. 109.

15. Arthur H. Rose, *Chemical Microbiology*, 3rd ed. (New York: Plenum Press, 1976), p. 403.

16. "U.S. Army Activity" in Senate Hearings, *Biological Testing*, p. 109.

17. Graham S. Wilson and Ashley Miles, *Topley's and Wilson's Principles of Bacteriology and Immunity*, vol. 1 (Baltimore: Williams & Wilkins, 1975), pp. 1100–1.

18. Bernard R. Davis, Renato Dulbecco, Herman N. Eisen, Harold S. Ginsberg, *Microbiology*, 3rd ed. (Hagerstown, Md.: Harper & Row, 1980), p. 709.

19. George A. Wistreich and Max D. Lechtman, *Microbiology and Human Disease*, 2nd ed. (Beverly Hills, Calif.: Glencoe Press, 1976), p. 316; Bob A. Freeman, *Burrows Textbook of Microbiology*, 21st ed. (Philadelphia: W. B. Saunders Co., 1979), pp. 172–73.

20. U.S. Department of Defense, "Biological Defense Program," Report to the Committee on Appropriations, House of Representatives, Washington, D.C., May 1986 (mimeographed), chap. 1, p. 10.

21. Carlton E. Brown, "Human Retention from Single Inhalations of Bacillus Subtilis Spore Aerosols," in *Inhaled Particles and Vapours*, ed. C. N. Davies, Proceedings of an International Symposium organized by the British Occupational Hygiene Society, Oxford, 29 March–1 April 1960 (New York: Pergamon Press, 1961).

22. Ibid., p. 126.

23. Ibid., pp. 130–36.

24. Ibid., p. 122.

25. Ibid., p. 137.

26. Ibid.

27. Ibid., pp. 137–38.

28. Richard P. Wheat, Anne Zuckerman, and Lowell A. Rantz, "Infection Due to Chromobacteria," *A.M.A. Archives of Internal Medicine* 88 (1951): 1.

29. "Information for Members of Congress," p. 5.

30. Victor L. Yu, "Serratia Marcescens, Historical Perspective and Clinical Review," *New England Journal of Medicine* 300, no. 16 (April 19, 1979): 887.

31. Ibid., pp. 887–90.

32. Charles Petit, "Bay Area Puzzle: Mysterious Surge of Heart Infections," *San Francisco Chronicle*, March 10, 1976; John Mills and Denis Drew, "Serratia Marcencens Endocarditis: A Regional Illness Associated with Intravenous Drug Use," *Annals of Internal Medicine* 84, no. 1 (January 1976): 32–33.

33. *New York Times*, March 13, 1977, p. 26.

34. Ibid.

35. "Information for Members of Congress," p. 9.

36. "Biological Defense Program," chap. 1, p. 11.

37. Senate Hearings, *Biological Testing*, p. 270.

38. Ibid., p. 261.

39. Ibid., p. 271.

40. Ibid., p. 285.

41. Ibid., p. 296.

42. *Assessment of Chemical and Biological Sensor Technologies*, a Report by the Committee on Chemical and Biological Sensor Technologies, Board on Army Science and Technology, National Research Council of the National Academy of Sciences (Washington, D.C.: National Academy Press, 1984), p. 70.

6

Airborne in the U.S.A.

Open Air Vulnerability Tests in Minneapolis, St. Louis, and the New York City Subway System

MANY DETAILS ABOUT the army's tests over populated areas remain secret. Most of the test reports are still classified or cannot be located, although a few of the earlier ones have become available in response to Freedom of Information Act requests and in conjunction with the Nevin case. Among those available, sections have been blocked out and pages are missing. Nevertheless, they reveal considerable information about the rationale and techniques of the army's program. The report dealing with the spraying of San Francisco in 1950 will be discussed in Chapter 7. Here we review excerpts from reports about subsequent tests in Minneapolis, St. Louis, and the New York City subway system.[1]

Although occasionally enlivened by comments about curious citizens or uncooperative local officials, in general the reports are dry and clinical. They are replete with lists of weather conditions, air currents, area maps, particle and bacterial counts, and the mechanics of dispersing and collecting particle samples. When viewed collectively, however, the reports provide additional impressions. In reading one report after another, the reader is astonished at the number of people who were exposed during the tests. Without exception, the reports disregard the potential health consequences to the millions of citizens exposed to the countless trillions of bacteria and particles. The determination to conduct these tests evidently overrode consideration of people's rights, as well. The reports unswervingly served these two themes: disregard of potential health hazards, and planned deception of the exposed human population.

There is no evidence that the officials who ran the tests intended to cause harm. But reference is never made to information available in the scientific literature that questioned the safety of the simulants.

59

Nor are the army's own memoranda mentioned concerning the possible harm caused by its San Francisco test in 1950.

In 1952 and 1953 (and possibly longer), a series of army studies titled "Behavior of Aerosol Clouds within Cities" described the spraying of several municipalities. Progress reports were prepared by the Army Chemical Corps every three months, and two of the reports, Joint Quarterly Reports numbers 3 and 4, covering January through June 1953, became available in 1980. Testing was conducted under army auspices in association with scientists from Stanford University and the Ralph M. Parsons Company of Pasadena, California.

Report No. 3 focuses on open air testing in Minneapolis during the first three months of 1953. Report No. 4 further discusses the Minneapolis test and describes new tests in St. Louis during the April through June period. The aerosol used in both cities was zinc cadmium sulfide, a fluorescent powder intended to approximate bacterial agents that might be used in biological warfare. The powder was sprayed from generators at various stations in the cities. Devices collected samples of air, and particle concentrations were assessed in laboratories by measuring the fluorescence emitted under a black light.

Joint Quarterly Report No. 3:
The Spraying of Minneapolis

The scope and objectives of the Minneapolis test "are part of a continuing program designed to provide the field experimental data necessary to estimate munitions requirements for the strategic use of chemical and biological agents against typical target cities," said the report. The objectives included determining "street level dosage patterns," the effects of "day and night meteorological conditions," and obtaining "data on the penetrations of the aerosol cloud into residences at various distances from the aerosol dispenser, and to determine whether there is any residual background or lingering effect of the cloud within the buildings."[2]

The last objective, with its interest in the "lingering effect" of the aerosol, hints that officials may have been interested in the effects of the particles on humans. But further reading dispels this idea. Nowhere are safety or risks to humans mentioned, and the lingering-effect phrase clearly refers to the length of time taken for the aerosol cloud to dissipate.

The report states that the "aerosol cloud study" included 61 releases of the fluorescent material in four areas of the city. Tentative conclusions are listed at the beginning of the report: First, "street-level dosage patterns are reproducible in an essentially residential area." Second, "similar patterns are obtained when the source is located at a street intersection, on a roof top, or in the middle of a block." Third, "of the penetration studies conducted in residences and in the Clinton School, greater degrees were obtained in the basements of houses than in the upper levels; in the school building, however, there was little difference in vertical distribution of the inside dosages" (p. 11). The experiment thus included massive exposure of people at home and children in school. Yet the human dimension is never mentioned, only clinical descriptions of the aerosol—its "penetration," "distribution," and "dosage." Who was breathing the material, and how much, seems to have been of no concern.

The report explains that operations during the three-month period in Minneapolis involved "81 field experiment hours and 11,170 man-hours, including full-time and part-time personnel in the field and laboratory." Experiments were conducted between 8:00 P.M. and midnight, and between 1:30 P.M. and 5:00 P.M. (p. 25). Thus hundreds of personnel were carrying out the experiments for months, when people were sleeping, at work, or commuting, when children were at school or playing outdoors. No time, no location, no segment of the population, whether old, young, sick, or poor, were exempt from exposure to the zinc cadmium sulfide particles.

A section of five pages of the report is titled "public relations," although in fact much is devoted to public deception. From the text:

> Advance meetings with the Mayor of Minneapolis, the Minneapolis City Council, and the Public Utilities Committee were held in August and September of 1952. . . . The result of these meetings was the extension of full cooperation of various city departments to the field office during the test program. . . . It was the desire of these departments to be prepared to dispel the anticipated concern of citizens calling to report unusual activities at unusual hours. [p. 26]

At a glance this passage might be taken to mean that the city officials were informed of the purpose and method of the testing arrangements. Careful reading of the remaining narrative indicates that this was unlikely. The officials evidently had been told that the tests involved efforts to measure ability to lay smoke screens about the city, because that was the story released by the army. The smoke-screen explanation was concocted to allay suspicions about the strange equipment and activities that passersby might notice. The misinformation effort included planting false news stories, like one cited by the report (on p. 30) that appeared in the *Minneapolis Tribune*: "Government research has shown that even in an age of radar-bombing, it may be desirable to hide cities with smoke screens in event of atomic attack. It is not known if any smoke has been released over Minneapolis. Several other cities also are involved in the tests."

The final paragraph of the report's section on public relations confirms the effectiveness of the army's deception. After the *Tribune* story appeared,

> other newspapers followed with reports of similar content. Public curiosity diminished rapidly following these press releases. However, to prevent further idle tampering or actual loss of equipment by theft, operators were furnished chains and locks with which sampling equipment could be secured to trees, lamp poles, or similar permanent objects. Few molestations of consequence occurred during the balance of the program. [p. 31]

Under the heading "equipment and procedures" is the description of the spraying process. A "continuous blower-type aerosol generator" released up to 3½ grams of fluorescent particles per minute for periods of at least 10 minutes. The generators were operated from the rear of a truck or from roof tops. "Full precautions are taken to avoid accidentally introducing contamination into the field office premises which would reduce the accuracy and reliability of particle counts" (pp. 22–23). Contamination was a concern, but only as it affected the army's particles, not the human subjects.

The lack of control after the particles were released is exemplified in the report's description of the sampling techniques. Membrane filter samplers were placed at specified locations to collect the airborne particles. But "should the wind shift after the initial release has been made, instructions are given either by direct contact or by radio to redistribute certain samplers." The image of operators grabbing samplers and racing to catch up with unexpected wind shifts is hardly one of scientific rigor. Nor is the report's observation that the filter surfaces "are generally faced downward in the event of rain." (pp. 23–24). This must mean they were sometimes faced up, which alone would affect the particle counts. None of these variables is explored, although the study is supposed to provide a scientific basis for army policy.

Toward the end of the report, dosages and penetration of the fluorescent particles are described. References are made to particle contamination in the Clinton School and nearby residences, as if only the physical structures were involved. Not a word appears about the humans who were breathing in the particles:

> Vertical samples taken outside windows of the first and second floor of the Clinton School, with other samples being taken on the roof, indicate a slight drop-off of dosage with altitude. A total of 48 samples were taken during 12 releases. Expressed as percents of the dosages

obtained at a sampler on the ground nearby, the median value for the first floor, second floor, and roof . . . were 93%, 88%, and 61.5%, respectively. . . .

Penetration into the interior of the Clinton School showed somewhat lower values. For 71 dosages obtained during the same 12 releases, the median values for the ground floor, first floor, and second floor were 23.5%, 27%, and 22.5%, respectively. The ventilating system of the school was not in operation during the tests.

Penetration into houses differed markedly from that at the school. Based on only 42 dosages obtained during seven releases, the median values for basement, first floor, and second floor were 13%, 11%, and 2%. Until further data are obtained it is difficult to account for the low value on the second floor. [pp. 37–38]

The further data mentioned in the last paragraph would be sought in later tests over Minneapolis and elsewhere; plans were already under way for additional spraying.

Joint Quarterly Report No. 4: From Minneapolis to St. Louis

The other available report in this early series of tests covered activities from April through June 1953. During this period, "necessary equipment was shipped from Minneapolis to St. Louis," where zinc cadmium sulfide was sprayed over residential, commercial, and downtown areas. "Of the 35 releases which comprised afternoon, predawn, and mostly nighttime operations, two were made on a citywide scale."[3]

As with the Minneapolis tests, the administrators of the St. Louis experiments were concerned that the public should neither question nor challenge their activities. Here too the test administrators sought the help of local officials. The report glosses over the point that at least one official apparently resisted (and perhaps was dismissed), saying only that "minor difficulties with the Park Commissioner were ironed out with the completion of the change in city administration." It noted further that "the public showed considerable interest" in some equipment, although "no incidents of consequence occurred" (p. 18).

Despite contacts by the test administrators with St. Louis officials, there is no evidence that these officials were better informed than their counterparts in Minneapolis about the true nature of the test and its potential dangers. Nor is there an explanation of the difficulties with the park commissioner or the incidents without "consequence" referred to in the previous paragraph. Uncertainty in this regard is joined by other unsettling characteristics. Not only was the manner of collecting particles for measurement questionable, as in Minneapolis, but an added difficulty is noted about the St. Louis experience:

> The tight labor market in St. Louis made it difficult to obtain adequate personnel, particularly responsible personnel. The scope of several of the tests was limited by the failure of employees to report for duty. It was necessary to discard some data because of obvious poor quality and incompleteness. The rapid personnel turnover, coupled with the generally disinterested attitude, made it extremely difficult to retain even a nucleus of trained people. [pp. 22–23]

These difficulties alone should suffice to raise questions about the validity of the St. Louis experiment. Yet the remainder of the report proceeds without a hint of doubt about the precision of its findings.

In discussion under "public relations," an intriguing comment is made about the smoothness of the St. Louis operation compared to that in Minneapolis. Oblique references are made to problems encountered in Minneapolis—lack of cooperation by residents, vandalism of equipment, and theft. The testers wanted to encourage more cooperation by the public in St. Louis than had been the case in Minneapolis. How to achieve this? Concentrate the tests in a poorer section of town and increase police surveillance. The testers theorized that poor people were less likely to object to strange happenings in their neighborhood, and if they did, the police would be there to control them. What else can be made of this passage:

> Much less public interest and curiosity was aroused by the field-test phase of the program in St. Louis than was experienced in Minneapolis. [The test area in St. Louis] consists principally of a densely populated slum district, and initial operations in this area were planned with particular precautions being taken in the arrangement of equipment and scheduling of manpower to minimize the possibility of loss of equipment. The Police Department requested that it be notified prior to each test in this area in order to be prepared to quell any disturbances resulting from the presence of the test crew in the area. While the nature of the district justified such precautions for each operation, the whole program was conducted without a single case of vandalism or disturbance. [p. 27]

The apparent lesson: to minimize chances of resistance to the performance of experiments, choose a slum where residents are less likely to be educated, inquisitive, or to question authority.

The report concludes with a series of charts, tables, and narratives that summarize findings of the tests in both cities. One item describes in detail several structures in downtown Minneapolis that were in the path of the aerosol releases. They include the telephone company, banks, office buildings, and medical facilities. This is the report's reference to one facility:

> Medical Arts Building. Located at 125 Ninth Street South, consists of two sections: the first, built in 1925, is 10 stories high, averaging 11,000 square feet per floor, and the second section, built in 1929, is 19 stories high, each averaging 5000 square feet. The building is constructed of reinforced concrete, with a brick exterior, and has one small basement and a sub-basement. It is well maintained and heated by vacuum steam. A fresh-air duct on the second floor is used in the basment. There are no storm windows in the building. [p. 50]

That is the entire description, not a word about the humans inside.

One of the final tables, in a section titled "Penetration," indicates how the sprayed particles would concentrate inside buildings. The table compares dosages inside and outside buildings at the same height (p. 65, Table III–6). Concentrations inside were as much as fourteen times greater, yet none of this seemed to phase the testers. Just as in the sterile description of the Medical Arts Building, the study ignores the fact that people were part of the experiment. No recognition is given to the fact that a medical building would house sick people whose illnesses could be aggravated by inhaling toxic particles.

The report mentions plans for more tests in the near future: a return to Minneapolis for additional testing in the summer, testing in Winnipeg, Canada, and intentions for "fluorescent-particle releases within the St. Louis industrial complex during the fall" (p. 7).

Miscellaneous Publication 25: The New York City Subway Test

Between the time of the spraying of Minneapolis and St. Louis in the early 1950s and the New York City subway system in 1966, scores of tests in other populated areas had taken place, as the army acknowledged in its 1977 report to Congress. Few details are known about the other tests, but the report on the New York City subway test confirms that the values behind the testing program had not changed during the years.

The army's attack on New York City in 1966 exposed more than a million people to bacteria called *Bacillus subtilis variant niger*. The report of the test, entitled "A Study of the Vulnerability of Subway Passengers in New York City to Covert Attack with Biological Agents," reviews a five-day period from June 6th through 10th when trillions of germs were released into the subway system during peak travel hours. The report's introduction provides the rationale for the experiment:

> A study of the vulnerability of a segment on a subway system to covert attack was undertaken to provide information on (i) agent distribution and concentration in order to assess threat of infection to subway passengers, (ii) ease of agent dissemination in the system, and (iii) methods of delivery that could be useful offensively. The subway lines in mid-town New York City were selected for investigation because of the heavy traffic and the number of lines available for tests.[4]

As with reports of the other vulnerability tests, there was no discussion of danger to humans who were breathing in the bacterial or chemical agents. The report remarks in passing that the bacteria were harmless, but it cites no evidence to support the claim (although it lists studies about aerosols and aerial warfare, includes the number of bacteria counted at various stations, and provides an exhaustive registry of subway car numbers). Nor was anything mentioned about the ethics of experimenting on unwitting subjects. On the contrary, the report indicates that every effort was made to deceive the public.

The testing was conducted by scientists and technicians (the number is not revealed), who unobtrusively dropped lightbulbs filled with the bacteria and charcoal particles into the subway system. The bulbs were shattered at sidewalk level on ventilating grills that opened into the system, or were tossed into the roadbeds as trains entered or left a station. Each lightbulb contained 30 grams of activated charcoal and 175 grams of the army's bacilli. The "viable count of the product was 5.0×10^{11} organisms per gram" or more than 87 trillion bacilli in each lightbulb. The charcoal darkened the agent and made the deposit less noticeable on the roadbed (p. 72).

Aerosol clouds were momentarily visible after a release of bacteria from the lightbulbs. "When a train was leaving the station, the cloud was pulled down the tube after it," according to the report, and "when one train was in the station the cloud covered it." How did the commuters react? "When the cloud engulfed people, they brushed their clothing, looked up at the grating apron and walked on" (p. 69).

Several tables elaborately review the "calculated respiratory exposure" of persons in trains and subway stations at various times and places. The tables list several downtown Manhattan stations and trains where calculations were made, and indicate that countless riders were breathing in many millions of the army's bacteria (pp. 56–65). One table, for example, indicates that on Wednesday June 8th, on the uptown platform at the 23rd Street Station of the 7th Avenue line, people were inhaling almost one million organisms per minute between the 5th and 10th minute following release of the bacteria (p. 60, Table 5).

Discussions about the test results reveal a consummate interest in the dissemination patterns of the bacteria. The narrative is, typically, clinical and dispassionate. One passage refers to "the penetration of agent into coaches and the exposure of people riding trains": "The times recorded for local train riders was 4 to 13 minutes, with the most frequent period ranging from 8 to 10 minutes. High exposure doses generally occurred within the first 40 minutes after dissemination. They were most frequent on local uptown trains" (p. 9).

Another paragraph refers to the dissemination pattern of the bacteria into subway stations:

> The data show that the agent aerosol was maintained in the target stations during a period of dissemination and was spread to stations along the tube by movement of trains. Distribution was similar to that from agent deposit, except that it was more limited because of the smaller quantity of agent disseminated. Agent was recovered in air sample in all but one station in the test on the Eighth Avenue line within 5 minutes after dissemination was initiated, and in all stations in the test on Seventh Avenue. Concentrations generally were highest in target stations and at nearby uptown stations on the uptown side and downtown stations on the downtown side. [p. 20]

If the health consequences of the tests were not on the minds of the investigators, the possibility of objections by the affected commuters was. The testing personnel were equipped with false letters of identification to assuage the concerns of curious bystanders:

> The several trials were conducted as completely independent operations without the knowledge or cooperation of the New York City Transit Authority or Police Department. Dissemination of agent and collection of air samples attracted no attention, and the tests were carried out without incident. Agent was disseminated without challenge or apparent detection. Air sampling was conducted more or less openly; it elicited few inquiries and no suspicion. Test personnel were given letters identifying them as members of an industrial research organization as a cover in case they were questioned. They were not used, except by one person who smoked in a station. He used his letter to prove nonresidency to a police officer. Following this, he completed sample collection without further questioning. [p. 22]

The disregard of people's health and right to know that they were serving as guinea pigs is colorfully demonstrated by the test administrators. A summary of their reports shows pride in having deceived their fellow citizens. Some treated an occasionally curious passerby with indifference, some with disdain. From the report of one tester: "Sitting on bench in 28th Street Station a man also sat on bench . . .

began to look at box sampler case . . . then asked me what was making so much noise. I answered . . . the . . . radio. He seemed satisfied. A train came in and he caught it" (p. 68; elipses appear in the report). From another: "A man sitting on bench beside me leaned over and looked into case. No comment made; I looked at him as if to indicate he should mind his own business and he looked away." From a third: "There were people who gave you the once-over or wanted to talk, but I went through the watch and writing act. That seemed to satisfy their curiosity, and I was too busy for conversation" (p. 70).

The army's conclusions from this study are as simple as the test was bizarre. The major finding: "Test results show that a large portion of the working population in downtown New York City would be exposed to disease if one or more pathogenic agents were disseminated covertly in several subway lines at a period of peak traffic" (p. 23). To reach this conclusion, the army exposed more than a million New Yorkers to countless trillions of bacilli, at a cost of unknown numbers of illnesses, deaths, and dollars.

Based on the experience of the test, the report suggests countermeasures against a germ warfare attack (pp. 26–27). Its six proposals range from the impractical to the surrealistic. First, "Include information on covert use of biological agents and likely ways of dissemination in the training of police and subway personnel." Does this mean passengers carrying lightbulbs would be under suspicion? Since germs could be dumped into the system in any number of ways, the proposal is vacuous. So is the second: "Instruct train operators, track maintenance, and other subway personnel to be alert and look for signs of covert use of biological agents during high risk periods." As well as uncertainty about what is meant by a high-risk period, looking for "signs of covert use" is as meaningless as the "likely ways of dissemination" in the first proposal.

The third proposed countermeasure is even more difficult to take seriously: "The ordinance against smoking in trains and stations is strictly enforced. Similar enforcement of an ordinance against litter would make clandestine deposit of agent in the system more difficult." While anti-littering ordinances may be more routinely violated than those against smoking, strict enforcement of the law could hardly make a difference during a germ warfare attack. The army's own experiment proved this. The testers were easily able to drop lightbulbs onto ventilator grills and inconspicuously toss them onto road beds. Not a single tester was questioned about his action. Amid the crowds and confusion during heavy traffic, it would be simple to drop bulbs or other containers without being noticed, no matter what an ordinance says about littering.

The fourth suggestion: "At critical political periods, an increase could be made in the number of station inspections, patrols of tracks, and trainmen on trains. Also, doors of coaches could be locked to prevent movement of passengers between coaches." What counts as a critical political period, the time around a presidential election? After a bellicose speech by a Soviet leader? The second instruction, locking the doors between coaches, would hardly prevent dropping germs into the system or exposing passengers. Unless the coaches were hermetically sealed, which would be impossible, bacteria would drift in from ventilator gratings, tunnels, and roadbeds.

The fifth proposed countermeasure: "Collection of air samples at one or more locations in downtown subway lines at peak workday traffic periods." How often? Which bacteria would be tested for? What would be done if an air sample contained harmful agents? None of these questions is raised, let alone answered.

Sixth: "Immunization of key personnel with vaccines available for potential biological agents and establishment of a volunteer immunization program for other workers. Vaccines exist for many potential biological agents, but are not generally used in this country. Mass immunization techniques have been successfully applied against natural diseases, such as smallpox and poliomyelitis."

If only "key personnel" are to receive vaccinations, what happens to the other passengers? Even if the millions of subway riders were to be included, questions abound. An effort to vaccinate citizens during the swine flu scare in the mid-1970s is instructive. Many people refused to be vaccinated, and several who were, suffered severe side effects. In the end, the predicted swine flu epidemic never occurred. The vaccination program was finally seen as a waste of money and an unnecessary risk to the recipients. The possibility of a germ warfare attack seems even more remote than the swine flu threat. A suggestion that everyone be immunized against an uncertain array of germ warfare agents is hardly likely to draw much cooperation.

In fact, none of the proposed countermeasures was implemented. The army must have recognized how silly they were, because no one ever talked about the countermeasures or the test to the police or subway authorities. The New York Metropolitan Transportation Authority learned about the test and the report when everyone else in the nation did, in 1980 as a result of a Freedom of Information Act disclosure.

Conclusion

The reports about the three tests place in doubt the value of the entire program of vulnerability testing. Whatever information may have been gleaned from the tests about air currents, dissemination patterns of particles and bacteria, or vulnerability of the public, is of questionable value in defending against a biological attack. Every proposed countermeasure that was formulated as a consequence of the New York City subway test is at best impractical. The most significant, if unintended, conclusion from the reports is that there seems to be no effective means to defend a large population against a biological warfare attack.

The United States remains a party to the 1972 Biological Weapons Convention, and that is comforting. But the Reagan administration's accusations that the Soviets have violated the treaty, and the consequent increase in funding for defensive biological warfare research, are worrisome. This is especially so in view of the army's position that open air vulnerability testing is an option within the terms of the treaty.

Another unintended lesson from the reports about the tests has to do with secrecy and bureaucratic inertia. Once the earlier testing program was underway, there was no stopping it. Doubts about safety during the program were minimized or ignored. Few people knew about the tests, and therefore few could raise questions about them. All the more, then, are citizens justified in seeking information about current testing practices.

Every "simulant" of lethal bacteria that was used in the tests was potentially harmful. This should have been recognized, as the previous chapter shows, because of information in the scientific literature before the testing program began. It became all-the-more obvious as additional evidence appeared in the scientific literature during the 1950s and 1960s. As will be discussed in the next chapter, consequences of the San Fransicso test alone should have raised enough concern to halt the program. There are indications that some who were associated with the program recognized the dangers. Yet the official line continues to be that such testing was and is harmless. No discussion about risks to the public appeared in any of the reports.

The third lesson relates to the question of ethics. The Nuremberg trials in 1948 had revealed details of the ghastly medical experiments conducted by German doctors on involuntary subjects during World War II. The judges' verdict included a list of principles that reflected the fundamental requirement of informed consent on the part of human subjects. Yet, in the following year, the army testing program began. None of the reports of the army tests includes a word about ethics or informed consent.

Sensitivity to the issue of experimentation involving unwitting subjects has grown in recent years, and institutional protections exist now where none did before. Yet protection of subjects during open air testing at present is more ambiguous than for human subjects in other types of research. Because the army's tests historically have involved exposing more people than has any other known experimental program, this is a paradox. The case of Edward Nevin, and the trial that it provoked, confirm that officials who run the testing program have not been particularly concerned about this issue.

Notes

1. I am grateful to Jeremy Paxman for providing the reports about Minneapolis and St. Louis, and to the Church of Scientology for the report about the New York City subway system, which they obtained through Freedom of Information Act requests.

2. "Behavior of Aerosol Clouds within Cities," Joint Quarterly Report No. 3, Chemical Corps, U.S. Army, January–March 1953, pp. 118, 119.

3. "Behavior of Aerosol Clouds within Cities," Joint Quarterly Report No. 4, Chemical Corps, U.S. Army, April–June 1953, p. 6.

4. "A Study of the Vulnerability of Subway Passengers in New York City to Covert Action with Biological Agents," Miscellaneous Publication 25, Department of the Army, Fort Detrick, Frederick, Maryland, January 1968, p. 7.

PART THREE
THE GOVERNMENT
ON TRIAL

7

Edward Nevin and the Spraying of San Francisco

O<small>N</small> D<small>ECEMBER</small> 22, 1976, Edward J. Nevin 3d was browsing through the *San Francisco Chronicle* while waiting for a train from Berkeley to his San Francisco law office. A reporter had just unearthed information that the army had secretly conducted a germ warfare test over San Francisco in 1950.[1] The bacteria had been implicated in the infection of several people and the death of one. Midway through the article, Nevin read that the deceased victim had been a retired pipe fitter, a patient who died at Stanford University Hospital on November 1, 1950. His name was Edward J. Nevin.

"I suddenly realized that they were talking about a story very close to me," Nevin recalls. As he learned of the strange circumstances associated with his grandfather's death, he says, "I felt incredible shock."[2]

Eddie Nevin's experience that morning was not unique. Says his cousin Philip Bray, "I thought, 'My God, that's *my* grandfather.' I hadn't thought about him for awhile—it was all in the past. And now suddenly the grave opened."

Eddie's younger brother, Inspector Michael Nevin, came upon the article at his desk in San Francisco police headquarters. "Years after he died, the family still talked about his suffering and the puzzle over what happened. When I saw the paper that all hit me." Most of the 67 descendants of the first Edward Nevin still live near San Francisco. By the end of the day, they all knew about the story.

Ed Jr., the youngest son of his immigrant parents, was 36 when his father died. He remembers the confusing circumstances surrounding the death. "He was recovering from an operation to remove his prostate gland. He left the hospital, and he went to my sister Ann's home in San Francisco to convalesce. And then it all started."

Ed Jr. speaks slowly. A college graduate, his gentle demeanor defies the stereotype of a retired policeman. He has spun the memory

75

many times but still seems incredulous. "My dad got very sick, and we took him back to the hospital. We went through that traumatic time because we didn't expect anything like it. Then, my father died." His voice becomes taut. "The doctors insisted on an autopsy. They apparently were as perplexed as we were."

The autopsy evidently did little to resolve the doctors' questions. The family was told that the death was from bacterial endocarditis, an inflammation of a heart valve caused by bacteria, but they learned little else.

Now the newspaper story revived the family's sense of frustration. Within days, Edward Nevin Sr.'s surviving son and four daughters gathered with their children in San Francisco. They wanted to learn more about their father's death and about the army test.

Philip Bray says, "We kind of looked to my cousin Eddie to take the lead, since he was a lawyer and worked in San Francisco." Eddie outlined the approaches the family could take. He explained the Freedom of Information Act. (It had been enacted two years earlier to help citizens obtain information from government agencies.) He considered which federal officials might be helpful, and whether congressional action might help the family's quest for information. Finally, he spoke about the possibility of suing the government. "Strange to say," says Ed Jr., "if my father had been part of the meeting, I think he would have spoken against suing. He would never have wanted to embarrass his adopted country." (Edward Nevin had been born in Ireland.)

How does a family determine to take the government to court, to risk condemnation as publicity-seekers? "A lot of us are still uncomfortable about the whole idea," says Joan Gallagher, a granddaughter of the elder Mr. Nevin. "Maybe Eddie and a few others liked the thought of publicity, but most of us didn't. We're really plain, unspectacular people." But everyone wanted to know more about the cause of death, and wondered whether the tests were still going on. All agreed that Eddie should seek more information.

Eddie and his wife had been planning a visit to Washington, D. C., in any case, and now he would call on government officials there about the family's concerns.

The Nevins versus the United States

The following month, Eddie met with congressmen, senators, and legislative aides. His discussions convinced him that neither requests to the army nor congressional hearings would yield the information the family and the public had a right to know. A second family meeting was held after he returned to San Francisco. Eddie told the group that he doubted if much more could be learned about the San Francisco test unless the government were brought to court. Everyone listened, probed, made suggestions. In the end, all agreed that suing seemed the only way to make the government respond.

Developing the grounds for a legal claim would take months. Eddie believed that the family should sue for an amount beyond anything they might hope to win. They eventually filed a claim for $11 million. After the trial in 1981 a reporter asked Eddie why the amount was so high. "Our motive all along has been to obtain information and tell the story. Would you fellows have paid attention if the claim were for only a few thousand?"

In 1977 Eddie filed suit on behalf of the 67 surviving children, grandchildren, and great-grandchildren of the first Edward J. Nevin, against the government of the United States. In response, the U.S. attorney's office in San Francisco asked that the claim be summarily dismissed on the grounds that the government was immune from suits by citizens. At that point a federal judge, still unknown to the plaintiffs, had been assigned to review the issue.

The basis of the government's request for dismissal lay in the notion of immunity that derived from English law and dated to a period when monarchs could not be sued by their subjects. English common law had been incorporated into the American legal system, and at one time citizens could not sue the federal government for any reason. Earlier in this century Congress modified this absolute immunity, but the government's attorney argued that the government in this case remained immune. He pointed out that the act of spraying the bacteria was part of basic policy determined at the highest levels. Such acts, even if they harmed people, were protected under the statutes.

If the request for dismissal had been granted, the case would have been over: no trial, no evidence in court. The cause of Edward Nevin's death would then have become officially irrelevant.

The government's request was returned with the word "Denied" stamped above the initials S. C. To Eddie, not only the decision but the initials were significant, for they meant that the judge assigned to the case was Samuel Conti. Although the case would be heard, Eddie was wary. Judge Conti, an appointee of Richard Nixon's, was a Republican conservative whose decisions were seen by many as influenced by his political passions. His record could not be encouraging to a plaintiff seeking to challenge the government. Nevertheless, the judge's refusal summarily to dismiss the case meant that the family would have its public hearing.

The trial date, initially set for 1979, was repeatedly postponed. Efforts to begin were frustrated by conflicts in the judge's or U.S. attorney's schedule, and then because of requests by the government for time to obtain information. In the end, the delays proved helpful to Eddie, for previously he had faced considerable difficulty in obtaining documents from the army. Though armed with the legal right to "discovery," Eddie had been continually frustrated by the army's insistence that reports were classified or could not be located.

Quite unexpectedly, beginning late in 1979, documents that had been classified or supposedly lost were made available. Eddie credits the turnaround to the newly assigned U.S. attorney, John M. Kern, who told him he wanted "a full and complete trial of the issues." Eddie thinks that Kern convinced someone in the Pentagon that "the only way of defending the case was to lay out all the documents." Eddie speaks with respect for Kern's efforts. A skilled and principled advocate, Kern was 33 years old when he was assigned to represent the army. His and Nevin's performances would later prompt a reporter to extol "the high quality of representation on both sides."[3]

The newly released documents helped amass previously inaccessible records. Information became available that went far beyond the limited issues of the Nevin suit. For purposes of the case, four documents were pivotal, three of which had not been available until the Nevin suit was instituted. The four documents represented principal reference points for the plaintiffs' arguments against the government.

Special Report No. 142: The San Francisco Test

Special Report No. 142 is titled "Biological Warfare Trials at San Francisco, California, 20–27 September 1950." It had been prepared in January 1951 and was kept secret until Nevin obtained a copy from the army twenty-nine years later. Although blocked out in several places by the army's censor, the report offers, through its charts, diagrams, maps, and narrative, a striking view of the San Francisco germ warfare test.

The report is introduced with an abstract that indicates that "a series of six experimental biological warfare attacks upon the San Francisco Bay area were carried out with nonpathogenic organisms during the period 20 through 27 September 1950. These attacks consisted of generating bacterial aerosols from a ship located at various distances offshore. The assessment of the degree of success of these attacks was made by means of aerosol samples collected at 43 locations throughout the San Francisco Bay area." The abstract contends that the bacteria used, *Bacillus globigii* and *Serratia marcescens*, were realistic simulants of organisms that might be used in genuine attacks.[4]

The test was "successful," according to the report, insofar as *Bacillus globigii* spores were detected in large numbers at the collection stations on the mainland. The fate of the *Serratia marcescens* was less clear, because "difficulty was encountered in making positive identification of the test organism" after spraying. The abstract concluded that the serratia probably survived but were difficult to detect because they might have lost their characteristic red pigmentation. The presumption was that "exposure of the organism to the elements caused it to lose its ability to pigment to its usual color."[5]

The body of the report began with a statement of the test's three objectives: to study "the offensive possibilities of attacking a seaport city with a BW aerosol" from offshore; "to measure the magnitude of the defensive problem"; and "to gain additional data on the behavior of a BW aerosol as it is borne downwind" (p. 1).

The week of testing involved the release for 30-minute periods of bacillus or serratia organisms along with fluorescent particles (zinc cadmium sulfide). *Bacillus globigii* were sprayed on four of the test days, *Serratia marcescens* on two. The mechanics of the aerosol generators are carefully described in the report, as are the types of filters and collectors at the sampling stations. Each of the six trials is reviewed separately, with careful accounts of the direction and speed of the wind, the course and speed of the ship, the time of aerosol generation, temperature, humidity, and bacterial counts at the sampling stations. Nothing is mentioned about monitoring the health of the human population or about the ethics of spraying unwitting subjects.

Excerpts from the report's discussion of one of the trials were typical of the rest. On September 25th, *Bacillus globigii* were released, forming a cloud about two miles long as the ship traveled slowly along the shoreline.

> The size and shape of the aerosol in this test approaches the ideal theoretical distribution of a cloud as it is borne downwind. Respiratory exposures were relatively high even on the eastern side of the bay, at those stations within the cloud pattern. . . . The maximum distance of effective travel measured in this trial extends inland to Station 43, approximately 23 miles from the aerosol source.
>
> The control samples collected prior to release of the aerosol, to determine the amount of residual airborne contamination, were all

essentially negative for the test agent. . . . Sampling was again continued
for an additional 2 hours beyond the normal sampling period at Station
31, and again a larger respiratory exposure was measured during the
later sampling period. [p. 24]

Calculations based on counts at sampling stations indicated that
many people were breathing in millions of the bacilli for hours after
the spraying. As indicated in the abstract, the consequences for the
serratia were less clear-cut. The sampling stations did not find evidence of large serratia counts shortly after spraying. Whether this was
because the organism failed to survive in large numbers, or simply
lost its ability to pigment, as the report supposes, is uncertain. The
latter seems plausible because "when the incubation period of the
collected organisms was extended to 4 days . . . a small percentage of
the organisms on the plates became pigmented to the usual color of *S.
marcescens*" (p. 36). This suggests that the serratia might have arrived
on the sampling plates in unpigmented form, but then began regain-
ing ability to pigment.

The body of the report ends with three conclusions (a fourth is
blocked out): First, "It is considered to be entirely feasible to attack a
seaport city with a BW aerosol generated from a ship or other source
located some distance offshore." Second, "The success or failure of
the attack would depend primarily upon the meteorological conditions at the time of the attack." Third, "Some additional useful data
were obtained insofar as BW and fluorescent particle aerosol travel is
concerned" (p. 39).

Appendices to the report included commentaries about the aerosol
generators, the samplers, and the fluorescent tracer particles that
were "released simultaneously" with the bacteria. In all tests

> the ships carrying the aerosol generating equipment moved from north
> to south during the release period, establishing a line source 2 or more
> miles offshore, and approximately parallel to the coastline. The release
> lane varied from 2 to 4 miles in length, but in each case was traversed in
> a 3–4 minute period. Generation of biological and fluorescent aerosol
> clouds was simultaneous and was maintained at a uniform rate during
> the release period except as noted in discussions of individual tests. The
> generators of the biological and fluorescent clouds were close enough
> to be considered a common source. [p. 45]

In a dispassionately worded summary, the report records that "San
Francisco was not as uniformly covered by the aerosol clouds as the
East Bay cities 10 miles beyond [but] nearly all of San Francisco
received 500 particle minutes per liter. In other words, nearly everyone of the 800,000 people in San Francisco exposed to the cloud at

normal breathing rate (10 liters per minute) inhaled 5000 or more fluorescent particles." Moreover, "the biological clouds released simultaneously with the inert aerosol covered very nearly the same area and presented similar dosage patterns" (p. 46).

Thus, using the army's data, nearly everyone in San Francisco inhaled not merely 5000 fluorescent particles, as the report says, but 5000 or more particles *per minute* during the several hours that they remained airborne. Since the army's bacteria "presented similar dosage patterns," San Francisco residents were inhaling millions of the bacteria and particles every day during the week of testing.

As was the case with the reports about tests over other cities and populated areas, Special Report No. 142 mentioned nothing about possible toxicity of the simulants, concern about informed consent by residents of San Fransicso and the Bay area, or the health effects on the people exposed.

The Wheat Article

The report of the San Francisco test would be useful in Nevin's trial preparation. But the document most essential to the family's suit was an article that had been in the open scientific literature since the time of the test. Its significance to the Nevin family was not recognized until information in it was mentioned in the newspaper story that revealed the army testing program.

In October 1951, an article titled "Infection Due to Chromobacteria" was published by Richard Wheat, Anne Zuckerman, and Lowell Rantz in the American Medical Association's *Archives of Internal Medicine*. The authors were from the Stanford University School of Medicine (Wheat and Rantz were physicians, Zuckerman a laboratory technician). They described an extraordinary epidemic of infections at Stanford's hospital in San Francisco caused by *Serratia marcescens*. Eleven patients were infected with the bacteria during a 6-month period beginning September 29, 1950.

The article was prompted by the fact that serratia infections had never before been reported at the hospital, and that despite intensive efforts by hospital investigators, the source of the infections could not be found.[6] The eleven patients ranged in age from 29 to 78 and all had undergone "some type of urinary-tract manipulation" involving the placement of catheters to enable them to empty their bladders.[7] The bacteria were isolated from urine samples, and in two patients from blood samples. One of these patients developed a bacterial endocarditis and died as a result. The article described the dead patient as E. N., a retired pipe fitter. It reviewed his medical history and indicated that an autopsy was performed to learn more about the unusual course of events.[8]

The serratia found in Mr. Nevin's heart was tested in a variety of ways, including for lethality when injected into mice, ability to produce its identifying red pigment, and resistance to antibiotics. Since all the hospital records concerning the serratia victims had routinely been destroyed in the 1960s, the Wheat article remained the only written documentation of the outbreak. Had it not been cited in 1976 by the newspaper reporter who first wrote about the army tests, the Nevin family might never have learned about it, and there would have been no suit.

Ad Hoc Committee Report

Another document with important implications for the Nevin case, and even more for the overall germ warfare program, was a two-page secret report on August 5, 1952, about the safety of the San Francisco test. Obtained by Nevin during pretrial discovery, it had been written by four scientists at the request of the Fort Detrick commander, General William Creasy. The scientists were asked to assess the possible hazards of spraying with *Serratia marcescens* in view of the Stanford hospital experience. They indicated that they met with officials at Fort Detrick, considered evidence concerning the Stanford outbreak based on the Wheat article, and "discussed the matter thoroughly." They recognized that although "an ideal simulant has not yet been found," *Serratia marcescens* had been commonly used previously to study "the dissemination of bacteria in the air."[9]

The scientists said that in the past there were "no reports of illness associated with this organism," but they agreed that there were such indications in "recent years." Their contention about no illnesses in the past is surprising in view of the many reports cited in the Wheat article that the scientists said they had read. The Ad Hoc Committee recommended that "on the basis of our study, we conclude that Serratia marcescens is so rarely a cause of illness and the illness resulting is predominantly so trivial, that its use as a simulant should be continued, even over populated areas, when such studies are necessary to the advancement of the BW program."

The committee's scientists made two recommendations that showed less than total confidence in their own advice. First, in view of the Stanford experience, "in future tests over populated areas, it would be desirable to institute prior and subsequent studies in a few hospitals." Second, Dr. Lowell Rantz, a coauthor of the Wheat article and an internationally respected epidemiologist, should "be cleared so that the full details upon which his published report is based may be made available for more thorough study." The report is signed by Victor H. Haas, M. Paul Hudson, Ralph E. Muckenfuss, and Alexander D. Langmuir. The scientists were civilians, but as was brought out in the Nevin trial, they were personally known to Fort Detrick's commander and apparently had worked previously in the army's biological warfare testing program.

Creasy's Response

The fourth centrally important document was a memorandum from General William Creasy. In response to the Ad Hoc Committee's report, General Creasy filed a letter with the chief chemical officer in the Department of the Army in Washington. Although important to the Nevin case, the letter's broader value lies in its revelations about the knowledge and attitude of the nation's germ warfare leaders. Creasy wrote that Dr. Rantz should be given security clearance, as the Ad Hoc Committee suggested. He noted that while *Serratia marcescens* would still be used in vulnerability tests, "caution [should] be exercised." Accordingly, Fort Detrick, the Creasy letter said, would consult with the U.S. Public Health Service to assess the effects on hospital patients in the areas covered by future tests.[10]

Creasy remained in charge of Fort Detrick for several years. By the time of his retirement seventeen years later, he was commander of the nation's chemical and biological warfare division. But as shown in the trial, Rantz was never given clearance, the Public Health Service was not consulted, and tests using *Serratia marcescens* and other organisms continued without a pause.

The trial, which had been repeatedly postponed during 1979 and 1980, was scheduled to begin on March 16, 1981. This time there would be no postponement. After the string of delays, an expenditure of $60,000 by the plaintiffs, and the emotionally draining years of preparation, Eddie Nevin could at last take the family's challenge to court.

In trials involving civil claims against the government, only a federal judge presides. Nevin would miss the jury, who he felt would have been less likely to exhibit bias than a single individual. On the other hand, he enjoyed a leeway available only in civil cases. He would not have to prove his case beyond a reasonable doubt, as in a criminal trial. He would have to show only "probability." If he could prove that the chances that the army's bacteria killed his grandfather were simply greater than 50 percent, he believed that would decide the issue.

When Edward J. Nevin 3d entered the courtroom on the first day of the trial, he was startled. The jury box was full. He quickly realized that it was occupied by members of the press. "How appropriate," he chuckled to himself. "The jury I really want to reach is the American people, and I'll be talking to them through the reporters in their seats."

The men and women in the jury box reached for their pens as the clerk announced Judge Conti's entry.

Notes

1. *San Francisco Chronicle,* December 22, 1976, p. 1. Drew Fetherston first reported about the army germ warfare tests in *Newsday* on November 21, 1976. In subsequent weeks he and John Cummings obtained additional information from the army, which appeared in *Newsday* on December 20th, and which provided the basis for the *Chronicle* article.

2. The comments and reconstructed dialogue in this chapter are based on interviews with members of the Nevin family in 1982 and 1983.

3. Jim Wood, in the *San Francisco Sunday Examiner and Chronicle,* March 22, 1981, Section 8, p. 6.

4. As explained in Chapter 5, *Bacillus globigii* is the same as *Bacillus subtilis.* Since the report of the San Francisco test refers to the organism as *Bacillus globigii,* we follow that usage in discussion of the test.

5. Special Report No. 142, "Biological Warfare Trials at San Francisco, California, 20–27 September 1950," U.S. Chemical Corps Biological Laboratories, January 22, 1951, p. iv.

6. Richard P. Wheat, Anne Zuckerman, and Lowell A. Rantz, "Infection Due to Chromobacteria," *A.M.A. Archives of Internal Medicine* 88 (October 1951): 6; see also Dr. Wheat's testimony in Chapter 8.

7. Ibid., p. 3.

8. Although E. N.'s age is listed in the article as 67, he was 75 when he died, according to members of the family. All other characterizations accord with what was known about the older Mr. Edward Nevin, and there is no question that he is the E. N. whose case is described.

9. Report of the Ad Hoc Committee to Brigadier General William M. Creasy, Commanding General, Army Chemical Center, Maryland, August 5, 1952.

10. Memorandum from Brigadier General William M. Creasy to Chief Chemical Officer, Department of the Army, Washington, D.C., August 22, 1952.

8

The Trial

AFTER JUDGE CONTI took his seat and called for opening statements, Edward J. Nevin 3d, for the plaintiffs, and John M. Kern, for the government, outlined the arguments they would pursue for the next two weeks.

Several surprises were to emerge in later days, but the facts that prompted the plaintiffs' suit remained beyond question: On September 26 and 27, 1950, the army sprayed clouds of *Serratia marcescens* from a boat off the coast of San Francisco. On September 29th, infections of patients with *Serratia marcescens* began appearing at Stanford University Hospital in San Francisco, the first ever recorded there. One of the infected patients, Edward Nevin, died as a result of serratia infection.

The Nevin family's case centered on three fundamental arguments: First, the bacteria sprayed by the army caused the death of their patriarch. Second, the army had ample reason in 1950 to suspect that *Serratia marcescens* could be pathogenic, and that spreading the bacteria over San Francisco was an act of negligence. Finally, the spraying of San Francisco with *Serratia marcescens* was not the kind of high-level government policy that would provide the government with immunity from suit.

Nevin offered his arguments in the context of his family's devotion to their country, a family who felt betrayed by their government's action. The Nevins were not radicals nor doubters, but grateful for what America had given them. He asked simply "on what basis in law does the government of the United States justify the dispersion of a large collection of bacteria over the civilian population in an experiment or testing program? Can there be any justification for exposure to risk, no matter what degree that risk, of a civilian population who has not given . . . any informed consent?"[1]

Nevin's opening statement summarized the allegations of negligence on the part of the army that he would try to prove during the trial. He concluded his remarks with the plea that the family of Edward Nevin seeks damage from this court for the untimely death of Edward Nevin, for the willful failure of the United States Army to obtain informed consent of any persons being exposed, and for the inadequate pretest investigation of the potentials for disease by that organism, for the willful failure of the United States Army to disclose to the plaintiffs what in fact had happened, for the nature and extent of the loss of that patriarch of that family. Thank you, your Honor. [pp. 37–38]

John Kern, the assistant U.S. attorney, was prepared to yield nothing. He would grant neither that the *Serratia marcescens* sprayed by the army was the same serratia that killed Nevin, nor that the army was negligent in using the bacteria in the first place. Contrary to the plaintiffs' claim, Kern argued that the bacterial warfare test was covered by the "discretionary function" exception. Thus the army was performing appropriately under official policy, according to Kern, and could not be considered culpable for damages in any case.

Kern recalled that American officials worried about the nation's vulnerability to biological weaponry during World War II and afterward. He took note of the committee that was established in 1948 to assess the vulnerability of the United States to covert biological attack. This committee, headed by Dr. Ira Baldwin, a distinguished microbiologist, proposed guidelines for a testing program. Kern acknowledged that the guidelines required that innocuous organisms be used in vulnerability tests, but he held that the San Francisco test met this standard. The possibility of harm seemed as unlikely, he said, as the possibility that "every atom in this pen could decide right now to rise up about six inches, and turn around 180 degrees." Since the planners and administrators of the test conformed to official policy, according to Kern, the government should be considered immune under the discretionary function rule.

Kern related how *Serratia marcescens* had been used during the 1940s in tests at the army's biological warfare laboratories in Fort Detrick, Maryland, prior to the large-scale outdoor program. People developed coughs and fevers, and some became concerned about its safety. As a result, a physician at Fort Detrick named Tom F. Paine conducted an experiment in 1946 using a strain of *Serratia marcescens* labeled 8 UK (so named because it had been sent originally from the United Kingdom). Kern told how Paine exposed four people to 2 million organisms per cubic foot for two and a half hours. He summarized the results: "When they got them out, there was some coughing, some redness of the eye. In fact, people developed a fever and all this occurred within two and a half, three hours. The durations of most of the symptoms were short-lived, i.e., a day, some symptoms on into the second day" (pp. 58–59).

Evidently these findings had not been sufficiently convincing to Kern, or to the army, to shake their view that the bacteria were really harmless. Kern concluded: "When you look at it in detail, you see to what extent they get ill, i.e., not an infection. You see that in even these massive dosages . . . the people got over it themselves with no treatment and the worst thing you had was a cough" (p. 61).

Kern then introduced a surprising thesis that would provide the basis of defense against one of Nevin's central charges. He would argue that the *Serratia marcescens* sprayed by the army and the *Serratia marcescens* that killed the elder Nevin were unrelated.

> You are talking about two completely different organisms. . . . The antibiotic resistances of the organism that infected and killed Edward Nevin are incredible, even with respect to the strains we are seeing today. It's incredibly resistant to just about everything. 8 UK is not, and the specific testimony on that will be offered . . . with a great degree of scientific certainty.

Kern contended further that the dates of appearance of *Serratia marcescens* at the hospital actually supported his thesis. The first case of serratia infection (Mr. Nevin's was the second) was cultured on September 29th, three days after the army began spraying the bacteria. This, according to Kern, was insufficient time for the organism to have gotten into the hospital environment and cause infection. He summarized: "So the testimony, then, from the government's point of view will be basically two ways. One, on the microbiological side, it is not the same organism. Two, from the epidemiological side, it couldn't happen in that time period" (p. 71).

Dr. Richard P. Wheat was the first witness to testify. The trial itself was possible only because of the article he had coauthored 30 years earlier. At the time that the epidemic occurred, Wheat was a young resident in internal medicine at the hospital, with a special interest in infectious diseases. The outbreak of the infections and the resulting death of Edward Nevin were so mystifying that Wheat joined with two other staff members to write about the incident.[2] The other two authors had died, and Wheat was now the only medical witness who had been personally involved with the episode.

Gray-haired, Wheat was still an active practitioner. He offered medical judgments with an effort toward objectivity, never in a way that suggested bias. He disclosed the frustration that he and his co-workers had felt thirty years earlier as they searched fruitlessly for the causes of the outbreak. They had been entirely unaware that the army had sprayed the area.

Nevin drew Dr. Wheat through the events from the time of his initial wonderment about the appearance of the bacteria in the hospital's patients, through the death of the elder Edward Nevin. What was it about the occurrences, Nevin asked the witness, that made it worthy of a medical journal article?

> Well, Serratia marcescens is an interesting organism which has been known from ancient times and, in fact, is one of the first bacteria we have records of. It's an important organism now, but at the time this article was written, it was a very rarely seen bacteria. It was a very rarely seen bacteria and very few reports had occurred in the literature. Our group of eleven patients were very unusual, and were very much worthy of reporting to the medical community. . . .
>
> The general feeling was this was a nonpathogenic bacteria, although when we began searching the literature at the time that these cases occurred, we found a number of references to human disease from this. [pp. 76–77]

This observation was important to the plaintiffs' contention that in 1950 there was sufficient literature to suggest the danger in using *Serratia marcescens*. Nevin emphasized the point by asking the witness: "As a result of your research in connection with the article, were you satisfied that the calling of Serratia marcescens a nonpathogenic organism was, in fact, inaccurate, and that was one of the motives for the article?" Wheat replied: "That is correct." He explained that he had spent many hours reviewing the medical literature on the subject in preparation for his article about the outbreak in his hospital.

Dr. Wheat then recounted the events that brought him to the elder Mr. Nevin. He met the patient when he was admitted to the department of medicine in August 1950 because he was having difficulty urinating. Nevin had been catheterized to relieve his problem and underwent surgery in September to remove his prostate gland. According to Wheat, Mr. Nevin recovered at the hospital during the following weeks. On October 1, toward the end of his convalescence in the hospital, he developed a "spiking temperature." A urine culture the next day revealed the presence of *Serratia marcescens*. Mr. Nevin was treated with antibiotics. The fever quickly subsided, and a few days later he was dismissed from the hospital. The dismissed patient stayed with his daughter for several days in San Francisco. It was evident to family members that he was becoming quite ill. At times he seemed incoherent, suffering increasingly from pain. He was readmitted to the hospital on October 11.

Now, thirty-one years later, Nevin's grandson asked Dr. Wheat what significance he attached to the fact that eleven patients had suffered serratia infections within a five-month period.

> Well, part of the interest in this particular outbreak was the fact that no similar organisms had been isolated in the hospital laboratory even as a curiosity. Then over a relatively short period of time there were a number of cases, four or five within a month, and then another five or six patients over the next six months. Then for reasons we didn't understand, the cases ceased, and that was a curiosity. [p. 86]

Dr. Wheat testified that he first learned in 1977 that the army had sprayed San Francisco in 1950. Nevin asked the doctor what he thought of the possibility of a "causal relationship between that spray and the outbreak at Stanford Hospital."

Wheat replied: "I think that it's very difficult for me to escape the conclusion that there is at least some probability, some causal effect that the serratia that was broadcast had some relationship to these cases, and I state that because we hadn't found it before, and that they did spray it in a reasonable period of time beforehand, and that the cases then disappeared (p. 93).

It was the answer Nevin had hoped for, and he turned now to the issue of negligence. He would next try to demonstrate through Dr. Wheat's testimony that the army should have known that *Serratia marcescens* was a risk to humans.

> NEVIN: Based upon your review of the report of the test and based further upon your background, training, experience, education as a physician, in your opinion were the people who planned the test in San Francisco from Camp Detrick, Maryland, required as a scientific requirement, to review the medical literature before determining that the selected bacterium was appropriate?
>
> WHEAT: I am not sure what they were required to do. I would hope that as scientists, they did review the literature, and I have no way of knowing whether they did.
>
> NEVIN: Assuming a review of the literature prior to 1950, would it be your opinion that the use of Serratia marcescens in this San Francisco test inevitably included some degree of risk?
>
> WHEAT: That would be my conclusion.
>
> NEVIN: And when we speak of risk there, are we referring to risk of disease in at least some few compromised hosts?
>
> WHEAT: I think that one would have to presume that that potential existed. The army was aware of that potential in terms of some of their previous writings.
>
> NEVIN: Okay. In light of your opinion that there was some inevitable risk in the use of the Serratia marcescens in the San Francisco experiment, do you have an opinion as a physician that there are some things that should have been done by the army that, in fact, were not done in the course of the testing procedure?

WHEAT: Well, hindsight is always grand, but I think that had I been on the army team, that I would have taken into my confidence, since this was not a super-high security problem, a few of the experts in infectious disease in the Bay area. I would have made them aware of what was going on, and asked them to report any problems which might relate to this to the army, so that a real body of knowledge could develop from this. It would be an incomplete test without that.

NEVIN: In your opinion, do earlier lab tests prior to 1950 on volunteers in the laboratory using the same organism have any real applicability to predicting the potential for spraying a population of 850,000 to a million people?

WHEAT: I do think they have inference. Inference was not taken by the army, nor by a great many other people as being significant. I think that was so because they were able to demonstrate the bacteria did circulate in the bloodstream, the bacteria were present in the urinary tract and so forth, after experiments, even though these were healthy people and bacteria caused no disease or illness.

NEVIN: Doctor, were you ever contacted by any member of the Ad Hoc Committee of 1952, which was charged with the investigation of the review of your article in order to determine whether or not there was a connection between the outbreak at Stanford and the test of the United States Army?

WHEAT: No, I was not. [pp. 95–97]

Dr. Wheat had provided the essential base on which Nevin would build the case.

Kern's cross-examination followed. He tried to get Dr. Wheat to acknowledge that articles written before 1950 about *Serratia marcescens* infections did not conclusively indicate the bacteria were harmful. But the doctor insisted that there was sufficient information to question the wisdom of wholesale spraying. Kern countered by affirming that the bacteria had been considered innocuous for years even after the San Francisco test and cited an experiment performed by Dr. Edward Kass in 1956 at the Harvard Medical School. Dr. Kass had exposed catheterized patients to *Serratia marcescens* so he could follow the path taken by bacteria causing urinary infections. "I would say that Dr. Kass took a calculated risk," Dr. Wheat commented (pp. 148–54).

Kern asked Wheat to quantify what he meant by risk. Wheat refused. "There isn't any way anybody can answer that. First of all, I don't know enough about Dr. Kass's bacteria or the patients or the methods or techniques of his procedure. Nor do I think anybody can put those kind of figures on virulence. There is too much individual variation among patients." Wheat then inquired whether Dr. Kass had informed the patients they were being used as experimental subjects.

"I am sure they were," Kern answered (p. 150). (One wonders on what basis Kern was sure, since no evidence was offered. If these patients were informed, this should have further served as a model for the army, although one to which it failed to conform. If informed consent was appropriate to Dr. Kass's patients, why not to the citizens of San Francisco?)

Kern moved from the question of risk to focus finally on that of probability of cause. After reviewing the dates that the army sprayed San Francisco, and the outbreak of infections at the hospital, he asked: "Can you offer an opinion with any medical probability on the question of whether the strain released by the army caused the infection?"

Dr. Wheat answered, "I can't say that it's a probability of 50 to 50.1 percent, and I don't know how you can say it's 32 percent or 76 percent. But I think the causal relationship has to be considered as a significant factor, and has to be thought of from a medical standpoint as being a probability until proven otherwise" (p. 171).

With these words Dr. Wheat had reaffirmed in cross-examination the plaintiffs' contentions on all counts. In 1950 he had personally researched the literature revealing problems caused by *Serratia marcescens*. No matter that some medical people continued to consider the bacteria nonpathogenic. Before exposing a million citizens to the bacteria, Wheat testified, army scientists should have thoroughly researched previous reports, as he had done. If they had, they should have recognized that the project would entail risks for many citizens.

Thus ended the first day of the trial.

The next day, William Haggard, a meterologist with the U.S. Weather Service at the time of the test, offered brief testimony about weather conditions in the test area. Haggard's principal contribution to the plaintiffs' case was his contention that testing in a populated area was unnecessary; the same information about dispersion patterns of bacteria could have been developed by spraying in uninhabitated areas (pp. 332–33). His testimony was followed by that of Edward Nevin Jr. (father of the plaintiffs' attorney) about his own father's benevolent character and the terrible impact of the unexpected death on the family.

The Germ Warriors

The first dramatic episode of the trial came on the third day with the appearance of Dr. Charles R. Phillips, a biochemist who had been chief of the Physical Defense Division of the biological warfare laboratories at Fort Detrick. Now retired, Phillips was the highest ranking official from Fort Detrick who was present at the San Francisco test.

Phillips testified that *Serratia marcescens* was not then, or ever, pathogenic. Despite reports about serratia infections and resultant deaths that appeared in the literature before 1950 and the increasing evidence afterward, Phillips insisted that "there is no known strain I am aware of that is considered pathogenic . . . today or yesterday" (p. 504). This contention by the scientist who had been in charge of the test prompted Nevin to ask, "If you were called on today and you were still in charge and not retired, would you approve of a spray of San Francisco with Serratia marcescens?" Phillips's response echoed beyond the courtroom into the next day's newspaper headlines: "I would."[3]

The other scientist who testified and who had been involved with the testing program was Dr. Oram Woolpert. Woolpert holds M.D. and Ph.D. (in microbiology) degrees, and was in charge of research and development on biological weapons at Camp Detrick. With his dual degrees he appeared unusually qualified to deal with the medical and scientific aspects of the biological warfare program. Yet, as with Phillips, his testimony seemed scientifically uninformed. He declared that nowhere in the literature, as far as he knew, had there ever appeared "a case of infection or pathogenicity" involving *Bacillus globigii*, another organism that was sprayed in the San Francisco test and many later ones.[4] (Contrary to Woolpert's supposition, as shown in Chapter 5, infections caused by the bacillus have been cited and recorded for years, including during the acknowledged period of army testing.)

In testifying about *Serratia marcescens*, Woolpert appeared as convinced as Phillips that spraying the germ was safe. He cited the study by Tom F. Paine conducted at Detrick in 1945, during which four healthy men breathed in large amounts of *Serratia marcescens* and ostensibly suffered no serious health consequences.[5] (The study in fact mentions that the men developed short-term fevers, chills, respiratory congestions, increased heart rates and blood pressure, and other untoward reactions.) Moreover, as Nevin elicited from the witness, no studies were done by the army to assess the effects of serratia on debilitated patients, or when the bacteria were introduced by nonrespiratory routes, such as through open wounds or the genito-urinary tract (pp. 853–54). Nor were there efforts to assess the bacteria's ability to resist various antibiotics, or to identify their infective potential (pp. 870–72).

Woolpert testified that in 1950 he was probably unaware of the studies that Dr. Wheat and others had cited in their article about serratia infections, although they had been reported for years before the San Francisco test. But even if he had known, he would have approved of spraying over populated areas. This, he reiterated, was because *Serratia marcescens* had previously been used at Detrick, and no one became sick. In any event, "I had a responsibility, high priority," he testified. "If I had not carried out my responsibilities . . . they could have done a lot of other things—put me in jail, I suppose" (pp. 884–85).

The two scientists appeared uneasy about having to justify their acts of patriotism. Although refusing to concede the possibility that the testing program was misguided, their demeanor was circumspect. Not so with the third character from that era who testified at the trial. Retired Major General William M. Creasy took the witness stand in dress uniform, with rows of decorations on his chest. He had been the senior military officer in control of all activities at Fort Detrick and all activities that emanated from the base. In testimony and attitude, according to courtroom observers, the general seemed to regard Nevin as a trouble-making recruit.

During questioning, Creasy habitually interrupted Nevin with observations such as "I don't get what it is you are trying to establish," "I don't see what problem is bothering you here," and "I am not swallowing . . . what you are trying to get me to swallow." When unhappy with Nevin's line of questioning he said defiantly, "You are wasting your time."[6]

Not once did Judge Conti chastise the witness for his comments. In fact, the judge appeared awed by General Creasy. This was not surprising to Jim Wood, a reporter for the *San Francisco Examiner*, who had been covering court cases for thirty years and knew of Judge Conti's fascination with the military. "When the government trotted out a witness in uniform," Wood said, "it was all over for Nevin.[7]

The judge's preferences remained unshaken even when Nevin exposed some of Creasy's testimony as untruthful. The general said that he favored arranging that Dr. Lowell Rantz of Stanford be given clearance after the serratia outbreak (confirmed in Creasy's 1952 memorandum, cited in the previous chapter). Rantz, an internationally respected scientist and one of the authors of the Wheat article, had had no knowledge of the army test. The purpose of the clearance would have been for the army's investigating committee to discuss with Rantz the possibility of a relationship between the army test and the hospital epidemic. The only reason Rantz was not contacted, according to Creasy, was that before anyone could "get him cleared or get more information from him, he died" (pp. 660, 669).

When Nevin confronted the general with documentation that Rantz did not die until twelve years after the test, Creasy became angry and said that his memory was no longer clear. Judge Conti summoned the attorneys to the bench where, according to Nevin, the judge admonished him for embarrassing the general. When the trial was recessed and Nevin walked outside the courtroom into the corridor, General Creasy stormed toward him and challenged him to a fist fight. Nevin retreated into the courtroom.

General Creasy, like Phillips and Woolpert, claimed that *Serratia marcescens* was a "completely non-pathogenic organism" (pp. 630–31). Nevin was able to demonstrate that Creasy, at least, had seen documents that questioned this supposition. Secret reports and correspondence among army officials shortly after the hospital outbreak were introduced as evidence, and Creasy acknowledged that he must have seen them at the time. The Ad Hoc Committee's report to Creasy (described in the previous chapter) said that "in future tests over populated areas, it would be desirable to institute prior and subsequent studies in a few hospitals to determine whether . . . the recovery of Serratia marcescens from patients was related to B. W. field tests."[8] When Nevin pointed this out to Creasy, the general said only that he found nothing in the committee's report "that indicates any continuing risk" (p. 669). The recommended studies were never undertaken.

In an apparent effort to emphasize the independence of the four scientists who comprised the Ad Hoc Committee, Creasy referred to them as "a group of outsiders" (p. 658). In fact, as Nevin elicited from Creasy, the general had known the scientists, and some if not all "had already been involved in the bacteriological warfare program" (p. 656).

The scientists who wrote the Ad Hoc Committee's report recommended that *Serratia marcescens* continue to be sprayed "even over populated areas." Yet, as their report makes clear and as Creasy admitted he knew at the time, the scientists never contacted any of the doctors at Stanford hospital, nor any of the infected patients or their relatives. They never examined any of the hospital records, nor cultures of *Serratia marcescens* taken from infected patients at the hospital. They made no effort to determine if the serratia sprayed by the army and the serratia that caused the infections were of different strains, as the army contended thirty years later. They made no effort to preserve for future reference any of the bacteria that had been cultured at the hospital. (Creasy's testimony that "there is nothing in this report that indicates any continuing risk," is close to the truth— because the authors of the report hardly sought to determine whether any risk existed.)

Creasy contradicted William Haggard's testimony that sufficient information could have been obtained by testing in uninhabited locations. The general emphasized that the vulnerability tests had to be done in populated areas, "because if you want to test the B. W. agent, the B. W. agent is designed to work against people, and you have to test them in the kind of place where people live and work" (p. 625).

Perhaps the most revealing comment about the army's attitude toward the public came during Creasy's response to a question about ethics:

> I would feel it completely impossible to conduct such a test trying to obtain informed consent. I could only conduct such a test without informing the citizens it was being conducted. I could not have hoped to prevent panic in the uninformed world in which we live in telling them that we were going to spread non-pathogenic particles over their community. 99 percent of the people wouldn't know what non-pathogenic meant, nor do any words I know appear to be such that you could get it across to them. [pp. 674–75]

Creasy, Phillips, and Woolpert are retired, but were they still in charge they would run vulnerability tests over populated areas as they did in the past, according to their testimony. This would involve using realistic simulants, calling them nontoxic (despite contrary evidence), ignoring the ethical norm of informed consent, and carrying out the tests in secret. As we shall discuss in later chapters, there seems little assurance that the thinking at biological warfare headquarters today is very different.

Following the testimony from the men who ran the earlier tests, the trial was largely devoted to the question of the likelihood that the army's germs actually caused the infections at Stanford hospital and the death of Edward Nevin. Contradictory testimony was offered by several scientists, none of whom had direct involvement with the biological warfare program. Most were not yet teenagers at the time of the San Francisco test.

The Plaintiffs' Expert

The first scientific testimony for the plaintiffs came from Dr. Stephen Weitzman, a specialist in infectious diseases. He criticized the army test on both scientific and ethical bases. From the scientific standpoint, it was "poorly designed, poor in scope, poor in the kind of questions they thought they might be able to answer." The test involved no control groups, Weitzman said, and there was no effort to obtain informed consent from the exposed population, though "there was, in 1950, definitely a known risk" (pp. 909–10).

Weitzman suggested that the detection techniques used by the army to determine the rate of survival and concentrations of *Serratia marcescens* during the test might have been too crude. He had seen the report of the San Francisco test and its indication of uncertainty about the bacteria's survival. "It could be that their method didn't work," said Weitzman; "there may have been serratia all around, but they just didn't have a sensitive enough technique" (p. 930). In any case it would not take many bacteria to create a large population rather quickly, he maintained, because "these bacteria can multiply every 20 or 30 minutes"; in addition, mutations or plasmid transfers can make bacteria resistant to particular antibiotics. (Mutations and plasmid transfers involve changes in the genetic characteristics of the organisms which are passed on to succeeding generations.) Thus in a short time the infective potential of the bacteria might become radically enhanced.

In view of the amazing coincidence of timing—the fact that serratia infections were recorded at Stanford hospital for the first time ever only a few days after the army test—Weitzman testified that "there was a very high probability that the army's experiment ultimately led to the death of Ed Nevin" (p. 985).

The Government's Experts

In response to Weitzman's testimony, the government presented two scientists who viewed the probability differently. Dr. John James Farmer, a microbiologist at the government's Centers for Disease Control, is an expert on *Serratia marcescens*. When he learned in the 1970s about the army test over San Francisco, he wanted to compare the army's strain of bacteria with the serratia reported in the Wheat article.

Wheat and his coauthors reported that they assessed the *Serratia marcescens* that had caused the hospital infections in a variety of ways. They tested the bacteria's resistance to antibiotics, its ability to kill mice when injected in various concentrations, and its ability to ferment or give off gas when placed in certain sugars.[9] Farmer was able to obtain from Fort Detrick a strain of 8 UK, the strain that the army used in the test. He tried to approximate the "fingerprinting" used by the Wheat group, that is, to run the same kinds of tests on the army's strain as Wheat had performed on the serratia that had caused infections.

Farmer testified that the 8 UK *Serratia marcescens* that he worked with reacted differently in the presence of sugar, that it was less resistant to antibiotics, and that although it could kill mice at high concentrations, it appeared less potent at weaker concentrations than the Stanford hospital serratia. He conceded that plasmid transfer could have occurred in which the 8 UK would have acquired pathogenic potential from other bacteria. He further acknowledged that a strain being transferred from patient to patient (as seemed to have happened in the hospital over a five-month period) could become "more virulent with time" (p. 125). Yet Farmer concluded that the chances that the army bacteria caused the outbreak were "less than one in one hundred" (p. 1252).

Nevin thought that Farmer's professed certitude would hurt the government's case. His 100-to-1 odds seemed unbelievable to anyone who was paying attention to all the testimony. As Nevin suggested during his cross-examination of Farmer, the 8 UK tested by Farmer might not have been the same as that used by the army thirty years earlier. This could happen because of imperfect preservation techniques or natural changes in succeeding generations. Furthermore, as Nevin showed, the Wheat article did not specify what culture medium was used to grow and observe the bacteria. Farmer could only guess that the medium he used was the same. None of these conditions seemed to faze Farmer, and he refused to qualify his virtual certainty that the army's serratia and the hospital's serratia were entirely unrelated.

The next government witness, Dr. Dennis Schaberg, also said the chances were remote that the army's bacteria caused the hospital epidemic. Schaberg, an infectious disease specialist with an interest in hospital infections, summarized his skepticism: "I think there are just a lot of very low frequency events that had to occur in series . . . for 8 UK to have caused this infection. It had to acquire resistance. It had to change its virulence properties, and then it had to gain access to the hospital" (p. 1584). Although such a sequence of events was unlikely, Schaberg agreed that the possibility of its happening could not be ruled out.

Schaberg, like Farmer, doubted that most of the *Serratia marcescens* released by the army in San Francisco harbor would have survived the two-mile drift to the mainland. The army report of the test, as Nevin pointed out, indicated that more than 700 trillion organisms were released. Only a small percentage would have had to survive to be able to gain a foothold in a conducive environment. During cross-examination, Schaberg calculated that under optimal growth conditions a single *Serratia marcescens* organism could multiply a billionfold in about sixteen hours (pp. 1627–29). He acknowledged, furthermore, that the genito-urinary tract of catheterized patients was particularly conducive to rapid growth of bacterial populations (pp. 1696–99). (This was precisely the route that was the suggested portal of entry of the serratia that infected Edward Nevin and the other ten patients at Stanford hospital.)

Schaberg unhesitatingly said he would advise against spraying populated areas today with any supposedly nontoxic simulant. But when Nevin asked him for his view about the wisdom of doing so in 1950, he was reluctant to answer. Nevin pressed him, however, and Schaberg agreed that in view of the scientific literature available at that time, an unpopulated location would have been preferable. The army could not have been happy to hear its witness say, "I think, at least my own personal opinion, that many of the answers that they wanted from this test could have been gained by doing the test" in an isolated place (p. 1645).

The most surprising aspect of Schaberg's testimony occurred not because of what he said, but because of an intervention by the judge. Near the end of Schaberg's cross-examination, Nevin questioned him about a different way of quantifying the possibility that the army's germs caused the infections. Prompted by a suggestion during a pre-trial deposition by Matthew Meselson, a Harvard molecular biologist, Nevin posed the following: Consider the ten years between 1945 and 1955 as 20 six-month periods. Consider also that Stanford University hospital was (and is) among the ten finest medical teaching institutions in the United States. Thus 200 half-year segments may be delineated (the ten best hospitals times the 20 six-month periods). In only one of the six-month periods and at only one of the hospitals were *Serratia marcescens* infections found. And this happened only a few days after the army had sprayed the area with *Serratia marcescens*. Nevin then addressed Schaberg: "So that in one six-month period it happened, didn't happen in any of the other 199. It happened in San Francisco where there was a spray prior to any outbreak." Therefore, Nevin asked, "Is not the percentage that it was chance .5 percent?" (p. 1670).

At that point Judge Conti interrupted and effectively put an end to Nevin's cross-examination of Schaberg. As the trial transcript shows, the judge seems to have taken the role of Nevin's adversary, asserting that other hospitals did not keep track of serratia infections or even recognize them (although no evidence was introduced to this effect). Nevin responded that even if the hospitals were not looking for serratia infections, the bacteria would have been found just as they had been at Stanford. The unique red pigment of the serratia would have shown on culture plates on which bacteria from patients' blood and urine samples were grown, as happened at Stanford. Judge Conti's attitude may be gleaned from the trial transcript:

NEVIN: But the clinical biologist is not looking for anything [in particular]. He is looking at a culture plate to see if there is a colonization of something from the body, taken from the body of a patient.

CONTI: You see, counsel, I asked for statistics the other day. I want to know what are the statistics on hospital outbreaks, when they are known to be Serratia marcescens type. That's all I am interested in. Is this the only one that ever happened? If it's the only one that ever happened, that's one thing. But I can't expect any concrete evidence because nobody kept track.

NEVIN: Your honor, a red serratia can be recognized. Why do we need . . .

CONTI: I don't care if it hits me right smack between the eyeballs. If they weren't keeping track of it, it doesn't make any difference.

NEVIN: But no witness can come in this court and tell you they didn't keep track of it.

CONTI: Well, I want to tell you one thing. That is not hard evidence that any court can base a judgment on.

NEVIN: If there is absence of an occurrence?

CONTI: If there is evidence they were not keeping track of it.

NEVIN: Where is that evidence?

[Nevin then tries to question the witness.] Let me ask you this, doctor. In response to the court's observations, if a patient were found to have an isolate of red pigment Serratia marcescens, which the hospital attributed to be the cause of the patient's disease some time prior to 1950, would you have expected that would have been reported?

CONTI: [addressing the witness] Do you know the procedures prior to 1950 in hospitals as far as reporting incidences?

(Witness shakes head)

CONTI: All right. You can't. That's what I thought. He can't testify.

NEVIN: Your honor, he can testify they wouldn't be reported.

CONTI: He can testify to one thing, but he can't testify to the other. He is testifying to a known fact that they weren't reported. You are asking him now to testify what the practice of the trade was at the time, and if he says he doesn't know the practice of the trade, he can't testify to it.

WITNESS: They were reported.

NEVIN: But were they reporting disease in the 1930s, '40s, and '50s? When a disease happened in a hospital, were they reporting the disease that happened?

WITNESS: I would expect so, yes.

NEVIN: Okay. When pneumonia occurred . . .

CONTI: Counsel, we are going to take a 5-minute recess. [pp. 1673–75]

With the call for recess, the judge ended the line of questioning. He simply would not let Schaberg respond to the possibility, as Nevin posed it, that the odds were 200-to-1 against the outbreak at Stanford hospital being attributable to chance. When Judge Conti asked Schaberg how he accounted for the fact that there were no serratia epidemics reported in hospitals before 1950 or for several years afterward, Schaberg could answer only, "I wish I knew. I wish I knew" (p. 1684).

Judge Conti's Final Intervention

In another surprising intervention, Judge Conti urged Kern to challenge the credentials of Nevin's final witness. Dr. Brian O'Brien, a microbiologist at a junior college in California, had taken the stand. Under Nevin's questioning, O'Brien indicated that he held a Ph.D. from the University of California at Berkeley, where he received an award in 1969 as the outstanding student in medical microbiology at the Ph.D. level. Although O'Brien's principal work had been with bacteria other than *Serratia marcescens,* Nevin offered him as an expert witness on what "laboratory experiments are able to produce or not produce; on the question of plasmid transfer; understanding in the field today of recombinant DNA and plasmid transfers, particularly regarding enteric bacteria, which are the kind of bacteria we are dealing with in this case; and for the state of the art of medical microbiology at the time in question, that is, 1950" (p. 1726).

Then, without any indication that the government's attorney intended to challenge the witness's credentials, the judge intervened. "I'll wait," said Conti, "until Mr. Kern *voir dires*" (p. 1726). *(Voir dire* is the legal term for inquiring into a witness's competence to testify.) The government's attorney immediately obliged. In response to the judge's prompting, Kern had O'Brien reconfirm that his research had not involved *Serratia marcescens,* and that his record of publications and academic assignments had been modest. Judge Conti then concluded that O'Brien was not "competent to testify on the subject matter that you [Nevin] elucidated that you would desire him to testify on, nor on the state of the art" (p. 1746).

In a rambling plea, Nevin told the judge that the questions he hoped to ask O'Brien dealt with "basic questions of science." O'Brien would be asked about the validity of comparing strains of bacteria when one strain is unavailable for examination, or of Farmer's supposed replication of tests when the original tests were incompletely described in a single medical article. "As to the state of the art," Nevin said, "who would be more appropriate to discuss development and state of the art than a teacher of microbiology . . . one who must, for the purpose of teaching, not only talk about today, but go back through the entire history of microbiology" (pp. 1746–47).

The judge would hear no more: "This witness does not satisfy credentials in order to testify in that regard. I am interested in science, not scientific legerdemain" (p. 1748). Nevin realized that arguing further about O'Brien would be unavailing.

Nevin was surprised, then, when the judge granted him permission to read as testimony the pre-trial deposition of Matthew Meselson, who could not be present. Meselson's research had not involved *Serratia marcescens,* yet if O'Brien's lack of work with serratia was the purported reason the judge refused to hear his testimony, why allow Meselson's? Nevin could only conjecture that this was a strange effort by Conti to compensate for the biases he had shown during the trial. Reading a deposition was a poor substitute for a live witness—it was too late to seek another scientific witness to replace O'Brien—but better than nothing.

Meselson's deposition added substantively to the arguments that had previously been advanced on behalf of the plaintiffs. As was evident from the dialogue read into the transcript, he was articulate and knowledgeable. His inability to attend the trial was surely a loss for the plaintiffs, assuming that the judge would have permitted him to testify in person. His deposition contained an impressive summary of biological principles and other considerations known in 1950 that the army had apparently ignored. Collectively they made the case that spraying San Francisco at that time, not to mention the rest of the country for years afterward, put many people at risk.

First, while *Serratia marcescens* in 1950 was not considered a cause of major health problems, the bacteria were then known to have caused "illness or infection." Second, as was well understood at the time, infection by an organism could depend on its portal of entry: "Eating it is one thing, breathing it is another, and introducing it in the urinary tract would be still another." Third, the form of the agent would be important, whether "in a liquid or dispersed in the air," and whether the particles could "penetrate and reach the depth of the lungs."

The fourth principle that Meselson cited as being understood in 1950, was that "response would be dependent on the dose." Bacteria that otherwise seem nonthreatening might in large doses cause serious health problems. Meselson's fifth point was a rejoinder to the army's citation of Paine's experiment in which four men breathed in large amounts of *Serratia marcescens* without apparently serious effects. "It's one thing to generalize from the exposure of two or three or four people; but it's another matter if you have to consider a population, let's say, of a million." Sixth, he pointed out that the "population of a city is extremely heterogeneous, genetically heterogeneous, but also in age and state of health." Finally, he noted that the principle of informed consent "was, of course, generally known and accepted" (pp. 1773–75).

Implicitly, Meselson found the army to have been inadequately attentive to any of these points. Taken together they appear to make a powerful case that the army's biological warfare testing program was scientifically, ethically, and medically unsound.

As to the likelihood of cause and effect between the San Francisco test and the hospital outbreak, Meselson's testimony included an elaboration of the model that Nevin tried to introduce when he cross-examined Schaberg. Noting that serratia outbreaks had never been reported at Stanford or other leading hospitals for years before and after 1950, Meselson said, "the coincidence in time and place is remarkable." He believed, therefore, that the burden to disprove a causal relationship lay heavily with the army, that weak or circumstantial arguments were inadequate. If the nation is to believe that there was no relationship, "we need something of a very forceful nature to disprove it" (p. 1835).

The Verdict

After Meselson's deposition was read, a few other items and depositions were recorded, and the attorneys made closing arguments. In essence, however, the trial ended with the reading of Meselson's testimony. Two months later, the judge delivered a 36-page decision. It surprised no one. On May 20, 1981, Judge Conti directed that judgment be entered in favor of the defendant.

The judge denied validity to each of the plaintiffs' claims. He concluded that the army's decision to test fell within the "discretionary function exception" to the Federal Tort Claims Act. That is, the United States could not be sued in this case because the decision to spray was part of national planning (which made it immune from suit) and was not taken merely at the operational level (which would have made it vulnerable to suit). He determined that the army exercised appropriate care in the choice of simulants. And he concluded that "any injury to plaintiffs was not the proximate or direct result of the release of Serratia marcescens, strain 8 UK, by the United States, its agents or employees."[10]

As Eddie Nevin left the court room he saw his father standing at the end of the corridor with a handkerchief to his eyes. He felt a wave of guilt for having put his father and the rest of the family through these years of ordeal. As Eddie drew close, his father embraced him, and told him how proud he was of how he handled the case. Months later, Ed Jr. told an interviewer that he never had second thoughts about the decision to sue and that his son "did a wonderful job." He said he wished the judge were less one-sided, "but I think we feel a lot of satisfaction that we kept the issue before the American people. At least we are all aware of what can happen, even in this country. I just hope the story won't be forgotten."

The Nevin family appealed Judge Conti's ruling, but a three-judge panel of the United States Court of Appeals, 9th circuit, refused to overturn the decision. On January 17, 1983, by a two-to-one majority, the appeals court judges decided that the government was immune from suit within the discretionary function exemption. The two judges would not consider "the possible risks of urban testing, and applicable medical concerns" because they did "not think this court is equipped to weigh [such] factors." The third judge held that the decision to test was made at the operational, not the planning level, though he was unconvinced that the army's bacteria had killed Nevin.[11]

Three months later, the family filed a petition for a hearing before the Supreme Court of the United States, but the court refused to consider the appeal.

Notes

1. Trial Transcript, *Mabel Nevin, et al., Plaintiffs, vs. United States of America, Defendant,* before Judge Samuel Conti, United States District Court, Northern District of California, No. C-78-1713 SC, March 16–March 31, 1981, p. 25. Unless otherwise noted, pages cited refer to this transcript.

2. Richard P. Wheat, Anne Zuckerman, and Lowell A. Rantz, "Infection Due to Chromobacteria," *A.M.A. Archives of Internal Medicine* 88 (1951).

3. "Scientist Testifies Germ Spray Was Safe: 'If you were in charge today, would you approve a test?' 'I would,'" *San Francisco Examiner,* March 19, 1981.

4. Trial Transcript, p. 721. *Bacillus globigii* is otherwise called *Bacillus subtilis* (see Chapter 5).

5. Tom F. Paine, "Illness in Man Following Inhalation of Serratia Marcescens," *Journal of Infectious Diseases* 79, no. 3 (1946).

6. Trial Transcript, pp. 652–55. Characterizations of the behavior of individuals at the trial are drawn from conversations with people who were present, including reporters, attorneys from both sides, and members of the Nevin family.

7. Interview with Jim Wood, court reporter for the *San Francisco Examiner,* February 5, 1982.

8. Report of the Ad Hoc Committee to Brigadier General William M. Creasy, Commanding General, Army Chemical Center, Maryland, August 5, 1952.

9. Wheat, Zuckerman, and Rantz, "Infection Due to Chromobacteria," pp. 5–6.

10. Judgment by Judge Samuel Conti, re *Mabel Nevin, et al., Plaintiffs, vs. United States of America, Defendant,* No. C-78-1713 SC, United States District Court, Northern District of California, May 20, 1981.

11. *Mabel Nevin, et al., Plaintiffs-Appellants, vs. United States of America, Defendant-Appellee,* No. 81-4365, United States Court of Appeals, Ninth Circuit. Argued and Submitted July 14, 1982. Decided January 17, 1983.

PART FOUR
NEW FEARS, OLD RESPONSES

9

Terror or Error: The Yellow Rain Puzzle

THE NEVIN TRIAL in March 1981 helped uncover information about the army tests that many people found reprehensible. Yet the activities had taken place years earlier and seemed largely of historical interest. Despite the army's unwillingness to foreclose the possibility of resuming open air vulnerability tests, few observers appeared worried. During the 1970s, vulnerability testing seemed unnecessary and unlikely. The 125 nations who signed the 1972 Biological Weapons Convention, including the United States and the Soviet Union, appeared to be adhering to its prohibition against developing, producing, and stockpiling biological or toxin weapons. Defensive work, which is permitted by the treaty, was largely limited to modest programs involving the development of vaccines and protective gear.

Two months before the Nevin trial, however, Ronald Reagan assumed the presidency on a foreign policy platform steeped in distrust of the Soviets. Before the year was over, the administration had accused the Soviet Union of violating several arms control agreements, including the 1972 Convention and the 1925 Geneva Protocol that forbids the use of chemical or biological warfare agents. During the next four years, charges about Soviet violations were raised with increasing frequency. By 1984, the possibility of resumed open air vulnerability testing seemed far greater than it had a few years earlier.

This chapter and the next assess the administration's view of Soviet biological warfare activities. The government's position has provided the basis for vastly increased budgets for research and development of defensive biological warfare capabilities, including a revived open air testing program.

* * *

The Reagan administration's conviction that the Soviet Union has been violating the 1972 Biological Weapons Convention is based on three sets of allegations. The first is that an anthrax epidemic in Sverdlovsk in 1979 resulted from an accident at an illegal biological weapon facility. Second, the Soviets or their surrogates used toxin weapons—"yellow rain"—in Southeast Asia and Afghanistan.[1] Third, the Soviets have been trying to develop new weapons by genetic engineering. Only the second charge, that involving yellow rain, has purportedly been confirmed by direct physical evidence.

Yet in this case, as in the other two, the validity of the government's claim has been vigorously challenged. In the early 1980s, newspaper editorials and op ed pages alternated between skepticism and support for the yellow rain thesis. While the *New York Times* was calling the government's case "inconclusive," the *Wall Street Journal* urged the United States to "reconsider its unilateral ban on the development of chemical and biological weapons."[2]

One observer insisted that "for all its shrillness, the government's case would not suffice to convict a purse snatcher." At the same time, another was impressed by the government's "*proof* that the Soviets and their proxies have murdered thousands of people in biological and chemical warfare" (original italics).[3]

Which of the two positions is correct? We may never know, but one point is irrefutable: the U.S. government has taken the position that its yellow rain accusations are beyond dispute. As discussed in this chapter, by ignoring weaknesses and inconsistencies in its "proof," the government's position seems to be influenced more by ideology than by sound evidence.

In addition to raising questions about the validity of the yellow rain accusations, the issue points to an inherently intractable question about biological warfare: How does one know if a biological warfare attack has taken place? If an epidemic suddenly occurs, even though the responsible organism is identifiable, its source may remain uncertain. Natural and indigenous processes continuously cause disease. Determining that a man-made contrivance is responsible may be impossible. That was precisely the focus of debate about the anthrax outbreak in Sverdlovsk. While the administration contended that the anthrax was spread as a result of an accident at a biological weapons installation, others noted that anthrax is endemic to the area. One student of the episode concluded that the outbreak probably resulted from the consumption of tainted meat.[4] Similarly, the government's insistence that the yellow rain mycotoxins in Southeast Asia were biological or chemical weaponry has been countered by the argument that these mycotoxins are naturally found in that area.

The Government's Case

The accusation that the Soviets were providing mycotoxins, specifically toxins from the fungus *Fusarium*, for use as weapons, was first made by Secretary of State Alexander Haig in September 1981. Two months later Richard Burt, director of the Bureau of Politics and Military Affairs for the State Department, graphically described the government's case. Before a Senate Foreign Relations Subcommittee in November 1981, he testified:

> Over the past five years, and perhaps longer, weapons outlawed by mankind, weapons successfully banned from the battlefields of the industrial world for over five decades, have been used against unsophisticated and defenseless people, in campaigns of mounting extermination, which are being conducted in Laos, Kampuchea, and more recently in Afghanistan. . . . These attacks were conducted by low, slow flying aircraft. . . . The plane would release a cloud, often described as yellow, sometimes orange, red, or other tints. The cloud would descend upon a village, or upon people in the neighboring rice paddies. The cloud seemed to be made up of small particles, which would make sounds, when falling on rooftops or vegetation, similar to that made by rain. It came to be called, by its victims, the "Yellow Rain." . . .
> [The exposed victims] would experience an early onset of violent itching, vomiting, dizziness, and distorted vision. Within a short time they would vomit blood tinged material, then large quantities of bright red blood. Within an hour, they would die apparently of shock and the massive loss of blood from the stomach.[5]

A hypothesis by government investigators that the causative agents were mycotoxins (trichothecenes derived from fungi) seemed, according to Burt, to explain the entire situation. The government contended that since such toxins cause these symptoms, and that trichothecenes are not found naturally in the combinations identified in the Southeast Asia samples, they must be toxin warfare agents. "The fit," said Burt, "was perfect."[6]

Several scientists received this contention with skepticism. Matthew Meselson, the Harvard molecular biologist, argued that the government's supposed facts were speculations. Contrary to the government's assertion, Meselson pointed out that "there is not even a single study of whether these mycotoxins do or do not occur naturally in Southeast Asia." In addition, he cited several studies that suggested that mycotoxins could not have caused the effects, such as rapid and massive hemorrhage and death, described by Burt.[7]

The State Department in March 1982 presented a lengthy report on the subject that sought to fortify the government's contentions.[8]

Ignoring the arguments of skeptics, Deputy Secretary of State Walter J. Stoessel, Jr., held a briefing about the report, and claimed categorically that "the Soviet Union and its allies are flagrantly and repeatedly violating international laws and agreements."[9] His uncompromising tone reflected that of the report, which declared that "the conclusion is inescapable that the toxins and other chemical warfare agents were developed in the Soviet Union, provided to the Lao and Vietnamese either directly or through the transfer of know-how, and weaponized with Soviet assistance in Laos, Vietnam and Kampuchea."[10]

The report was based largely on testimony of individuals who said they experienced attacks, and on evidence from physical samples taken from sites where attacks allegedly occurred. The government contended that the Soviets or their surrogates employed a variety of chemical and toxin weapons. In explaining why the government could offer little tangible evidence, the report stated: "Collecting samples possibly contaminated with a toxic agent during or after a chemical assault is difficult under any circumstances, but particularly when the assault is against ill-prepared people without masks or other protective equipment." Moreover, trichothecene toxins "may be diluted by adverse weather conditions to below detectable concentrations."[11]

The report acknowledges that of fifty samples of materials taken from Afghanistan and Southeast Asia in alleged attack areas, none contained known chemical or biological warfare agents, and only four (later raised to five or six) contained "high levels of trichothecene toxins." The inability to find known agents in any sample, and trichothecenes in so few, was attributed to the lack of persistence of the materials over time.[12]

Despite the scarcity of physical proof, the report concludes that the information provides "compelling evidence" that Lao, Vietnamese, and Soviet forces had been using "lethal chemical and toxin weapons" since the mid-1970s.[13] In February 1983, the State Department was still insisting that "toxin weapons are being used right now in Afghanistan and Southeast Asia."[14] A year later the administration indicated that the use of chemical and toxin weaponry had declined, and might have ceased, as a result of America's public disclosure of the issue.

The Ember Article

Nowhere has the weakness of the government's case been better documented than in a comprehensive article by Lois Ember in *Chemical and Enginnering News*. Ember, a senior editor of the journal, reviewed every piece of alleged evidence cited by the government through 1983—from the physical samples through the testimony of alleged victims and eyewitnesses. Her conclusion: "The U.S. simply has not proved that toxin warfare has taken or is taking place in Southeast Asia or in Afghanistan."[15]

Ember first outlines the core of the government's case: that trichothecene toxins do not occur naturally in Southeast Asia, and that the combination of these toxins found in physical samples and in samples of the urine, blood, and tissues of purported victims came from man-made (Soviet) weapons. Yet, more than 90 percent of all the samples tested revealed no traces of toxins. In Ember's words, "the grand total of positive physical evidence gathered by the U.S. is slight: five environmental and 20 biomedical samples (including some tissues from an autopsy) from Southeast Asia, plus one contaminated gas mask from Afghanistan" (p. 10).

The thesis that trichothecene toxins produced by *Fusarium* fungi were being used as battlefield weaponry was evidently introduced by Sharon Watson, a toxicologist at the Armed Forces Research Center. A leaf taken from an area in Kampuchea following an alleged attack in March 1981 was given to Chester J. Mirocha, a plant pathologist at the University of Minnesota, who confirmed the presence of trichothecenes. After this the government began giving Mirocha other samples taken from areas of alleged toxin attacks. In addition Joseph D. Rosen, a food scientist at Rutgers University, reported finding toxins in a scraping of yellow powder from Laos, powder provided by ABC news. Ember comments on these incidents:

> The U.S. has tested about 100 environmental samples for trichothecenes. Mycotoxins have been found in five samples collected from sites of alleged attacks in Laos and Kampuchea. All control samples collected from areas near but not at attack sites have been found to be toxin-free. William Sarver, chief of the methodology research team analyzing yellow rain samples at the Army's Chemical Systems Laboratory, has not identified a single toxin in any of the myriad samples he has tested. All positive U.S. environmental (and biomedical) samples have been reported by Mirocha. Other than Mirocha, only Rosen, who analyzed a nongovernmental sample, has reported the presence of toxins. And directly or through an intermediary, Mirocha has received all his samples from Watson.
>
> Why Mirocha, according to Watson, is batting five-for-six in finding toxins in environmental samples from Southeast Asia, whereas Sarver is batting about zero-for-60 is yet to be explained. [p. 12]

Ember reviews the results reported for each of the five samples from Southeast Asia and finds that they are not "scientifically impressive" (p. 16). A sample allegedly from an attack in Kampuchea in March 1981, for example, was split into two sections that gave different readings. The sections differed not only in amounts of various trichothecenes, but in ratios of one toxin to another. Another sample from the same alleged attack showed still different combinations of toxins, and some of the trichothecenes found in the previous sample were entirely absent from the second. The other samples revealed dissimilar ratios and contents as well. Ember finds it difficult to believe that every positive sample of ostensibly Soviet-manufactured toxin should vary so much from the other in ratio and content (pp. 16–18).

As for evidence that toxin weapons were used in Afghanistan, a gas mask apparently purchased by U.S. agents in Kabul in September 1981 was found to contain a trichothecene toxin "on the outer surface, but not on the filters," Ember reports. Another mask and environmental samples from Afghanistan revealed no trichothecenes. She indicates that the "single gas mask is the sum total of the government's physical evidence for toxin chemical warfare in Afghanistan" (p. 19).

Ember then assesses the reports about blood and urine samples from alleged victims of toxin warfare attacks. Samples were collected from sixty people who complained of symptoms that the government associates with yellow rain attacks, including vomiting, skin irritation, and hemorrhagic (bleeding) abnormalities (p. 14). Twenty were said to contain traces of trichothecenes. Ember notes that "positive samples often have been collected one to 10 weeks after an alleged attack, yet animal studies indicated that these toxins are almost entirely flushed from the body within 48 hours of exposure" (p. 20). In addition, she points out that the government has never discovered a mode of delivery of these supposed toxin weapons. No associated bombs, casings, or shells have ever been found. Nor, apparently, has the government tested the food eaten by the refugees, which may contain the *Fusarium* mold and account for the trichothecene findings in their specimens.

Ember then reviews three other phenomena relative to the subject: first, the significance of the presence of pollen in all the samples; second, inconsistencies in the statements from alleged attack victims; third, the improbability of the use of trichothecenes as a weapon when far more effective agents are available.

The finding of pollen in yellow rain samples led Sharon Watson, the government's original proponent of the toxin-weapon hypothesis, to theorize that the Soviets purposely mixed pollen and some kind of solvent with the toxins. The solvent would enhance the toxin's "going through the skin," according to Watson, but whatever remained on the surface would dry, and with the help of the pollen become aerosolized, breathed in, and "retained in the bronchi of the lungs." This toxin-pollen-solvent combination Watson called a "very clever mixture" (p. 22).

Matthew Meselson became curious about the Watson thesis and began to consult scientific colleagues who were experts about insects and plants in Southeast Asia. Several confirmed that the pollen samples were from plant families common in Southeast Asia, and that the pollen is gathered by bees. Thomas D. Seeley, a Yale professor and Southeast Asia bee expert, noted that the report of finding concentrations of yellow spots conformed with the dropping of feces of the honeybee while in flight. Meselson then compared photomicrographs of yellow rain with those of locally collected bee excrement. He found them remarkably similar in appearance and in pollen counts. Moreover, all the spots exhibited considerable diversity of pollen types (p. 23). This may not have conclusively proved that yellow rain was bee excrement, said J. Perry Robinson, a British chemical and biological warfare expert who teaches at Sussex University, but "on the evidence that there is around, [this was in 1983] the bee theory is as good as any other theory" (p. 24).

Ember turns to analyze the "150 to 200 reports" compiled by the State Department about purported yellow rain attacks among the Hmong tribesmen of Laos. She notes that virtually all the reports came from a refugee camp in Thailand whose leadership is "composed of former members of the old CIA-backed secret army in Laos" (p. 29). Almost no other Hmong made claims about being subject to chemical or biological warfare attacks. Moreover, individual accounts vary widely from one person to the next, and even by the same person over time. One refugee, Ger Pao Pha, had testified extensively before the press and U.N. and other investigating teams. He described an attack in 1978 during which he once claimed 230 people from his village died. Later, to another group, he said 13 died. Still later, the number became 40 (p. 30). Erratic and inconsistent accounts, Ember demonstrates, were common among other refugees as well.

In assessing the manner of interviews and the refugees' responses, Ember consulted several social scientists and Southeast Asia experts. Each concluded that the refugee reports seemed unreliable, and that the refugee accounts did not make the case for the government's claim. They pointed out that the U.S. interviewers did not take into account cultural differences between themselves and the Hmong interviewees, that the interviewees may have tried to please the Americans with answers they wanted to hear, and that individual stories were not cross-checked for accuracy.

Jeanne Guillemin, an anthropologist at Boston University, makes an elementary observation that might account for the responses of the Hmong. The American interviewers apparently "didn't appreciate the vulnerability of the people being interviewed, that they were refugees who did not want to spend their life in a camp in Thailand. Of course they are going to be accommodating. Who wouldn't?" (p. 32).

Finally, Ember makes the point that if the Soviet Union wanted to use chemical or biological warfare agents, trichothecenes would be a poor choice. If the intent were to annihilate an enemy, many more potent agents are available. If it were to terrorize people and make them ill, more controllable agents, such as the riot gas CS that was imployed by U.S. troops in Vietnam, could be used. The use of riot agents, moreover, evidently does not violate international treaties (p. 26).

Growing Skepticism

Shortly before the Ember article appeared, a committee of the National Academy of Sciences issued a report on *Protection Against Trichothecene Mycotoxins*. The report was prepared by a panel of distinguished scientists at the request of the army. While the scientists do not criticize the government's thesis, neither do they endorse it: "The committee neither supports nor refutes the evidence for the military use of mycotoxins in embattled areas."[16] The committee issued the disclaimer that such a consideration was not part of its charge. Yet the report's conclusions make clear how little is known about the toxins or their effects on humans, which raises further doubt about the government's certitude. From the report:

> Current research programs do not address the persistence of trichothecenes in nature and the hazards of long-term exposure to these toxins. In addition, there is little information on the chemical behavior of mycotoxins in soil and waters, and their uptake by plants, or their transfer through food chains. Studies are not known to be underway to determine the periods of resistance of mycotoxins in waters and soils. No studies have been conducted on the leaching, degradation in nature, or products formed in waters and soils following treatment with trichothecenes, and there are essentially no data on any other mycotoxins.[17]

Saul Hormats, a former director of the army's chemical weapons program, was less equivocal. Writing in early 1984, he noted that if the Soviets wanted to attack a village with biological or toxin agents, yellow rain mycotoxins would be a silly choice. If the aim were to kill, a half-pound solution of botulinal toxin "would kill everyone in a village if the poison was released in or near it." If the intention were to incapacitate, spraying staphylococcal enterotoxins from a few small cans would make most of the villagers "extremely ill for a day or two." In both instances the cause would appear to be food poisoning. Other biological agents, Hormats points out, could be just as effective and would require a munition weighing as little as two ounces.[18]

Hormats then describes what would be required for the yellow rain toxins to be equally effective:

> Compared to these agents, yellow rain presents tremendous logistical problems. Yellow rain itself has been reported by the State Department to contain only very small percentages of the supposed toxic ingredient, called T-2. Since one part yellow rain is reported to contain only one ten-thousandth part or less of T-2, and T-2 is only one-fiftieth as toxic as our present lethal chemical agents, it would take some 300,000 tons as much fusarium mold to attack a given target than if a standard lethal chemical agent were used. At a minimum, about 3,000 tons of yellow rain would be required to attack a village. To place this quantity on the target would require 20,000 to 30,000 shells . . . or a minimum of 8,000 tons of bombs dropped from the air.[19]

Hormats notes that at this level of firepower targeted villages would have been physically obliterated, and this did not happen. The other assumption is that "the agent was delivered as a cloud from large transport or cargo planes." Hormats finds this equally unconvincing, because the mycotoxin is a solid, not a gas or volatile liquid. "To be effective, it would have to be dropped from an aircraft as very finely divided particles and then inhaled by the people in the village. But if the necessary 3,000 tons was dropped in this way over a village, very little of the light, fluffy material would reach the target. Most of it would be carried away by the wind."[20] Hormats concludes that the yellow rain issue is "ludicrous."[21]

Philip Boffey, a science reporter for the *New York Times*, summarized the arguments for and against the yellow rain thesis that had been advanced through mid-1984. He noted that the purported physical evidence was growing older; the government had produced no new environmental samples in 1983 or 1984, and found poisons in the urine of "only two supposed victims of such attacks." Nevertheless, the government would not retreat from its position. It surmised that the Soviets had merely switched to less potent agents.[22] Boffey cites the claims by proponents of either side of the yellow rain question and tries to present an unbiased account. Yet he raises questions about whether trichothecenes were accurately identified in the first place:

> When the United Nations conducted an investigation in 1981, it sent specimens of yellow powder and vegetation from Laos to three top

laboratories in three countries. At the same time, it sent samples that were know to be spiked with trichothecenes and samples that were known to be blank. Two of the laboratories failed to find any trichothecenes, even in the spiked samples. The other laboratory said it found trichothecenes in all of the samples, including the blank.[23]

None of this budged official thinking in Washington. In a 1984 report on *Soviet Military Power*, issued about the same time as Boffey's analysis, the Department of Defense stated unequivocally that the United States had "strong evidence of the actual use of chemical and toxin weapons by the Soviet Union and its client forces in Afghanistan, Laos and Kampuchea." In support of this contention, the report indicated that a "group of agents, known as mycotoxins, has been identified in the laboratory from samples collected in Afghanistan."[24]

In fact the only physical sample from Afghanistan that showed trichothecenes was a single gas mask; five purported environmental samples were from Southeast Asia. Beside mixing up the location of the contaminated samples, the report failed to mention that the overwhelming majority of samples from areas supposedly under toxin attack showed no mycotoxins. Nor did it note the inconsistencies in virtually every other category of purported evidence.

The government's theme was promoted by some commentators, none with more enthusiasm than William Kucewicz, an editorial writer for the *Wall Street Journal*. During April and May, he wrote an 8-part series, titled "Beyond 'Yellow Rain'—The Threat of Soviet Genetic Engineering." The articles ranged across a wide spectrum of alleged Soviet biological warfare activities, which are dealt with in the next chapter. The yellow rain allegations, as far as the author was concerned, were beyond dispute. Without a hint that the evidence was ambiguous or that several scientists rejected the government's contentions, Kucewicz called yellow rain "the best-known demonstration of the active Soviet biochemical military program."[25]

Kucewicz's imbalances and inaccuracies were addressed in a critique in the *Bulletin of the Atomic Scientists*.[26] But the most convincing scientific arguments against the yellow rain thesis were developed by five scientists in a 1985 *Scientific American* article. Some of the scientists had been quoted in the Ember article the previous year, and much of what they now wrote was an elaboration of points made by Ember. In the interim, however, they scrutinized the records of interviews conducted with alleged witnesses and victims of toxin attacks, they assessed the reports of trichothecenes toxins in samples, and they evaluated the yellow material itself that was collected from alleged attack sites.[27]

The article cites gross inconsistencies in the 217 interviews that were reviewed. Secretary of State Haig had claimed in his 1981 statement that symptoms of victims of yellow rain attacks "commonly included skin irritation, dizziness, nausea, bloody vomiting and diarrhea and internal hemorrhaging." The interview records indicate that only 8 percent of the respondents reported having bloody vomiting, 10 percent having bloody diarrhea, and 21 percent having rashes or blisters. More than three-fourths of the respondents had none of the supposedly common symptoms, and only 8 of the 217 reported the three symptoms in combination, either in themselves or other alleged victims. "Remarkably," says the article, "the frequency of reported illness is as high among respondents who describe arriving at a site after an attack as it is among respondents who were allegedly exposed directly."[28]

Other reasons for skepticism about the validity of witnesses' accounts are reviewed as well. Interviews were conducted with refugees who claimed in advance that they had been victims or witnesses. Randomly chosen refugees from the same village, which would have provided a cross-check, were not sought out. Thus, as suggested in the Ember article, the interviewing technique reinforced uncertainty about the credibility of the refugee reports.[29]

The second area of skepticism concerned the reports of trichothecene toxins in samples. The *Scientific American* article reviewed the discrepancies between reports by laboratories that examined environmental samples from alleged attack sites. It refers to the five positive samples found by Chester J. Mirocha of the University of Minnesota, and the one by Joseph D. Rosen of Rutgers University. Yet of more than eighty environmental samples from alleged attack areas tested for trichothecenes by the army's laboratory, not one proved positive. "There is little doubt about the Army's ability to detect trichothecenes," the authors note, because "control samples intentionally contaminated with trichothecenes have consistently yielded positive test results." The authors wonder if the few positive test results on environmental samples could have been the result of experimental artifacts or whether the "authenticity and integrity of the samples" had been compromised.[30]

The third area of challenge, the nature of the yellow rain material, amounted to an expansion of the hypothesis suggested two years earlier that yellow rain is the feces of Southeast Asia honeybees. Sharon Watson, the government scientist who first proposed that yellow rain was an enemy weapon, derided the bee hypothesis as "perhaps the most amusing" challenge to the government's position.[31] Nevertheless, the article elaborated on the argument previously set forth by one of its authors, Matthew Meselson, who originally proposed the bee hypothesis. The article indicated that every sample containing trichothecenes also contained large varieties of pollen. Experts were cited who noted that the "plant families in the yellow rain pollen could be identified with certain families strongly represented in Southeast Asia," and that "the flowers of these plant families are frequently visited by bees."[32]

Testing of the yellow rain samples and of honeybee feces showed equally high concentrations of pollen, about a million pollen grains per milligram. Other findings common to both materials included components of bee hairs, bits of fungi, and similarly appearing morphologies and varieties of pollen. The most dramatic incident involved a visit to Southeast Asia by three of the authors (Seeley, Meselson, and Akratanakul) in March 1984. The scientists undertook a field study in Thailand of honeybee nesting areas and found large swaths of yellow-spotted vegetation which they determined to be fecal deposits. At one point they were actually caught in a fecal shower.

> We were visiting a region known for bee trees in which an unusually large number of nests are suspended. In the village of Khua Moong, about 24 kilometers south of Chiang Mai in Thailand, we examined the area around two such trees, one bearing about 30 nests and the other more than 80, hanging from 20 to 50 meters above the ground. As we observed the second tree through binoculars from a clearing about 150 meters away, we saw a lightening in the color of several nests. Hundreds of thousands of bees were suddenly leaving their nests. Moments later drops of bee feces began falling on and around the three members of our party. About a dozen spots fell on each of us. We could neither see nor hear the bees flying high above us. . . .
>
> Our observations showed that showers of honeybee feces do indeed occur in the Tropics of Southeast Asia; moreover, the showers and spots closely resemble the showers and spots said to be caused by yellow rain.[33]

The three scientists later visited the refugee camp where most of the interviews with witnesses of the alleged yellow rain attacks had been conducted. One of the three (Akratanakul) speaks Lao, and the scientists were able to question sixteen groups at random. After the groups were shown leaves spotted with bee feces, thirteen groups "concluded they did not know what the spots were, although some people said they had seen such spots before." Two groups, totaling fifteen people, said the spots were "kemi," their term for the chemical/ biological warfare poison. One group of three people also agreed the spots were "kemi," although one of the members initially thought the spots might have been insect feces. The authors concluded that the Hmong refugees from Laos do not "generally recognize honeybee feces for what they are," and that some think the feces are agents of chemical or biological warfare.[34]

The *Scientific American* article represented a culmination of growing skepticism about the government's view of yellow rain. It prompted Nicholas Wade, an editorial writer for the *New York Times* who specializes in science affairs, to write that "Yellow rain is bee excrement, a fact so preposterous and so embarrassing that even now the Administration cannot bring itself to accept it."[35]

Government officials responsible for monitoring yellow rain developments refused to comment on the article, although one said he had seen a draft and found little new in it.[36] The Reagan administration's pronouncement of yellow rain, reiterated in a report to Congress in February 1985, remains official policy. The Soviet Union, according to the report, continues to be involved in the "production, transfer and use of trichothecene mycotoxins."[37]

Notes

1. Toxin weapons are the chemical products of organisms used for military purposes. They have been variously defined as biological weapons, chemical weapons, or something between. Toxins are given the same status as biological agents, however, under terms of the 1972 treaty. Their development, production, or stockpiling "for hostile purposes" is no less a violation than that for bacteria, viruses, or other living organisms. See *Convention on the Prohibition of the Development, Production and Stockpiling of Bacteriological (Biological) and Toxin Weapons and on Their Destruction*, Opened for Signature at London, Moscow, and Washington, April 10, 1972, Article 1.

2. *New York Times*, December 3, 1982, p. A–30; *Wall Street Journal*, September 2, 1981.

3. Gene Lyons, "What 'Rain'?" *New York Times*, March 3, 1982; and Dan Quayle, "Soviet 'Yellow Rain' Is Real and Devastating," *New York Times*, March 16, 1982, p. A–22.

4. Raymond A. Zilinskas, "Anthrax in Sverdlovsk?" *Bulletin of the Atomic Scientists* 39, no. 6 (June–July 1983): 26.

5. Jamie Kalven, " 'Yellow Rain': The Public Evidence," *Bulletin of the Atomic Scientists* 38, no. 5 (May 1982): 16.

6. Ibid., p. 17.

7. Ibid.

8. U.S. Department of State, *Chemical Warfare in Southeast Asia and Afghanistan*, Special Report No. 98, Report to the Congress from Secretary of State Alexander M. Haig, Jr., March 22, 1982.

9. *New York Times*, March 23, 1982, p. A–1.

10. *Chemical Warfare in Southeast Asia and Afghanistan*, p. 6.

11. Ibid., p. 7.

12. Ibid., p. 8.

13. Ibid., p. 6.

14. U.S. Department of State, *Yellow Rain: The Arms Control Implications*, Current Policy No. 458 (Washington, D. C.: Government Printing Office, February 24, 1983), p. 1.

15. Lois R. Ember, "Yellow Rain," *Chemical and Engineering News* 62, no. 2 (January 9, 1984), p. 34. Unless otherwise indicated, the following references in this chapter are to this article.

16. *Protection Against Trichothecene Mycotoxins*, Report of the Committee on Protection Against Mycotoxins, Board on Toxicology and Environmental Health Hazards, National Research Council of the National Academy of Sciences (Washington, D. C.: National Academy Press, 1983), p. 1.

17. Ibid., p. 90.

18. Saul Hormats, "A Chemical Warfare Expert Who Doubts the Soviets Used Yellow Rain," *Washington Post*, February 26, 1984, p. D–1.

19. Ibid.

20. Ibid., p. D–4.

21. Interview, September 13, 1985.

22. Philip M. Boffey, "Evidence Is Fading as U.S. Investigates Use of 'Yellow Rain'," *New York Times*, May 15, 1984, p. A–1.

23. Ibid., p. B–6.

24. U.S. Department of Defense. *Soviet Military Power, 1984* (Washington, D. C.: Government Printing Office, 1984), p. 70.

25. William Kucewicz, "Beyond 'Yellow Rain'—The Threat of Soviet Genetic Engineering," *Wall Street Journal*, April 23–May 18, 1984, specifically April 23, 1984, p. 30.

26. Leonard A. Cole, "Yellow Rain or Yellow Journalism?" *Bulletin of the Atomic Scientists* 40, no. 7 (August–September 1984): 36–38.

27. Thomas D. Seeley, Joan W. Nowicke, Matthew Meselson, Jeanne Guillemin, and Pongthep Akratanakul, "Yellow Rain," *Scientific American* 253, no. 3 (September 1985): 128–37.

28. Ibid., p. 130.

29. Ibid., pp. 130–31.

30. Ibid., p. 131.

31. *New York Times*, August 12, 1985, p. A–13.

32. Seeley, Nowicke Meselson, Guillemin, and Akratanakul, "Yellow Rain," p. 133.

33. Ibid., p. 137.

34. Ibid.

35. Nicholas Wade, "Rains of Error," *New York Times*, August 30, 1985, p. A–24.

36. *New York Times*, August 12, 1985, p. A–13.

37. Wade, "Rains of Error."

10

Engineering Genes for Defense

Recombinant DNA Technology and Biological Warfare

The New Biology

IN 1972, THE YEAR when the Biological Weapons Convention was signed by the United States and the Soviet Union, Janet Mertz was planning to undertake an unusual experiment. A graduate student in molecular biology, she was working under the supervision of Professor Paul Berg at Stanford University. When Mertz joined Berg's laboratory group in 1970, experiments were underway involving a virus called SV40, which was known to cause tumors in animals. Her project would be to try to integrate the genetic material (DNA) of the virus with that of the bacterium *E. coli*. The hope was that as the bacteria reproduced, they would continue to express the genetic material of the virus.

Mertz mentioned her impending project to the instructor of a course she was taking on cell culture techniques at Cold Spring Harbor in 1971. The instructor, a cell biologist named Robert Pollack, raised the question of possible hazard. Since *E. coli* are common inhabitants of the human gut, he wondered if bacteria altered by Mertz might not find their way into humans, who would then be endangered by the bacteria's ability to produce the genetic material of the cancer virus. After discussing the project with several other scientists, Mertz became increasingly concerned:

> I made the decision not to do the experiment, even though I was quite upset about the whole matter and was thinking to myself, "Well, here is a really good thesis project that I've gotten started on and these guys are telling me I can't do my project." On the other hand, coming from a radical-type background, I figured, "Well, even if it's only a [slight] chance that there's actually something dangerous that could result, I just don't want to be responsible for that type of danger." I started

thinking in terms of the atomic bomb and similar things. I didn't want to be the person who went ahead and created a monster that killed a million people. Therefore, pretty much by the end of that week, I had decided that I wasn't going to have anything further to do with this project, or for that matter, with anything concerned with recombinant DNA.[1]

Mertz told Berg about her discussions, and during the following months he consulted with other colleagues. Many expressed concerns similar to Mertz's, and he decided to suspend his laboratory's efforts to recombine DNA. Berg soon joined with several scientists to call for a comprehensive assessment of the potential problems. This was the genesis of a series of dialogues and conferences during the 1970s about the wisdom and safety of research involving recombinant DNA (sometimes called gene splicing or genetic engineering).

The implications of recombinant DNA work for biological warfare were quickly recognized. Bernard Dixon, an editor of *New Scientist,* wrote in 1973 that aside from other possible problems,

> DNA hybridisation must also look an attractive proposition for biological warfare researchers (who are, of course, still about their business, despite recent gestures toward biological disarmament). The new technique offers the prospect of fabricating ever nastier BW agents, facilitating the combination of "desirable characteristics" that cannot be brought together by conventional microbial genetics.[2]

Dixon did not amplify on his claim that biological warfare researchers were "still about their business," but his concern was echoed by several scientists. In 1974, preparations were begun for an international conference on the subject of hazards from recombinant DNA research, to be held in 1975 at Asilomar in California. Distinguished molecular biologists would be invited to assess the entire range of potential dangers.

An organizing committee established several panels of scientists to help formulate an agenda for the conference. One panel, called the Plasmid Working Group, was to consider the potential dangers of gene splicing involving bacteria and plasmids (small, circular segments of DNA often found inside bacteria). The group considered a variety of issues, such as genetic exchanges known to occur naturally, the likelihood of inducing pathogenicity in organisms, and the possible ecological effects of the experiments. It proposed six classifications of experiments, ranging from those in which biohazards would clearly be insignificant to those "judged to be of such great potential severity as to preclude performance of the experiment, under any circumstances at the present time."[3]

The report of the Plasmid Working Group concluded with a

statement about what it thought to be the most alarming prospect about genetic engineering:

> We believe that perhaps the greatest potential for biohazards involving alteration of microorganisms relates to possible military applications. We believe strongly that construction of genetically altered microorganisms for any military purpose should be expressly prohibited by international treaty, and we urge that such prohibitions be agreed upon as expeditiously as possible.[4]

Despite the report's admonition, no discussion about the implications of genetic engineering for military purposes took place at the 1975 Asilomar conference. Many scientists evidently felt satisfied that the 1972 Biological Weapons Convention precluded the need for further consideration of the matter. The focus of concern had become so concentrated on the general issue of protecting the public's health, that conference leaders believed military considerations were only incidental to the larger safety issue.[5]

During the next few years this attitude persisted. The safety of recombinant DNA research, but not its military implications, was argued across the country—at municipal meetings, in Congress, in universities, among scientific societies. The National Institutes of Health issued a series of guidelines shortly after the Asilomar conference that established safeguards in proportion to the perceived hazard of an experiment. Some research was prohibited entirely, as suggested by the Plasmid Working Group and endorsed by the plenary body of the conference. By the end of the decade, some of the restrictions were relaxed. A consensus had emerged in the scientific community about the safety of most recombinant DNA work, based in part on knowledge that emerged from ongoing experimentation.

In the 1970s, articles and books on the subject were written by a variety of observers: scientists, social scientists, philosophers, lawyers, journalists. Some were steeped in scientific arguments, some emphasized the history of the debate, some supported the research, and some did not. Yet virtually all ignored the issue that seemed so important to those who raised it in the first years of the debate—the military applications of genetic engineering.[6]

The pattern continued into the 1980s. The safety of recombinant DNA research in general no longer seemed alarming to the public. The few scientists who continued to express concern did not mention the military implications. Liebe Cavalieri, for example, a molecular biologist who had written and spoken extensively during the previous decade about the potential hazards of recombinant DNA research, reviewed his thoughts in a book in 1981. He was still worried about the safety of gene splicing, as well as its "social and often philosophic" implications.[7] Yet despite the breadth of his concerns—from the effect on ecological balance to accidental or purposeful alterations of evolutionary patterns—he mentioned nothing about the use of genetic engineering for military purposes. The subject seemed to be a non-issue.

Awakened Concerns about Genetic Engineering and the Military

In 1982, attention was suddenly revived. Jonathan King, a molecular biologist at the Massachusetts Institute of Technology, was among the first to readdress the issue. In remarks at a symposium on chemical and biological warfare sponsored by the American Association for the Advancement of Science, and in an article titled "The Threat of Biological Weapons," King linked his concerns to the state of world conditions.[8] He noted that East–West relations were deteriorating, that many nations had still not signed the Biological Weapons Convention, and that the Reagan administration had accused the Soviet Union of violating the Convention. The charges of violations related to the anthrax outbreak in Sverdlovsk in 1979, and "yellow rain" that was supposedly being used in Afghanistan and Southeast Asia.

The administration had not yet claimed that the Soviets were engaged in genetic engineering for military purposes; that would not come until 1984. But King was concerned that the U.S. Army had already incorporated recombinant DNA research into its research program. In 1980, the army had advertised in *Science* magazine for proposals "on the introduction by recombinant DNA methods of the human nervous system gene of acetylcholinesterase from human neuroblastoma cells into a bacterium. The purpose of the research is to obtain a microorganism which synthesizes the human enzyme so that it can be isolated for biochemical, neurochemical, and pharmacological studies."[9] Proposals were to be sent to the U.S. Army Research and Development Command at Fort Detrick, Maryland. The advertisement demonstrated that the army's biological warfare program now included an effort to manufacture the enzyme acetylcholinesterase. The action of the enzyme, which is essential to the transmission of nerve impulses, is blocked by nerve gases.

The army also had received permission from the National Institutes of Health advisory committee on recombinant DNA to engage in other toxin research. It would seek to clone certain toxins by genetic engineering technology, and try to introduce the gene for pneumococcus toxin into *E. coli*.[10] This was the kind of experiment that had set off the initial recombinant DNA debate a decade earlier, when Janet Mertz decided not to introduce cancer virus genes into the same bacteria.

The army's program involving recombinant DNA for military purposes had begun at least three years before the Pentagon announced that the Soviets had one. The government's later claims—that Soviet genetic engineering activities demonstrated its untrustworthiness—consequently were less persuasive. Howard Zochlinski, a biomedical researcher and science writer, visited the army's research facility for infectious diseases at Fort Detrick in 1982. Despite assurances by an army spokesman that recombinant DNA research there was "strictly in the realm of medical treatment," Zochlinski found that some of the research had unspecified "ominous overtones." His article concluded with the hope that congressional oversight would continue to ensure "non-involvement with biological weapons."[11]

About the same time, Sheldon Krimsky, a social scientist at Tufts University, published an assessment of the relationship between social responsibility and recombinant DNA research. In one section devoted to the issue of biological weapons, he raised questions of increasing concern: "What assurances are there that rDNA technology will not be used by the Department of Defense to produce new biological weapons or improve conventional ones? . . . Is there a clear distinction between offensive and defensive biological weapons? Does it even make sense to speak about defensive biological weapons?"[12]

Krimsky could only speculate. He referred to a report issued in 1980 as part of the review process established by the 1972 Biological Weapons Convention. The review committee had determined that recombinant DNA techniques were covered by the Convention's prohibition of offensive biological weapons development. This evidently meant that a nation could legitimately use the techniques in conjunction with "defensive" research. Yet, as virtually everyone who is knowledgeable about biological warfare research recognizes, the line between offensive and defensive is unclear. It depends on the scale of the work being undertaken and on the intention of the scientists doing the work. Especially since provisions for outside inspection are absent, the matter rests largely on trust.

In the end, Krimsky asked, "How can public skepticism be turned into public confidence?" He answered by emphasizing the importance of three existing institutions that he believed vital to the effort. The first is the 1972 Convention, however imperfect. The second is a law that supposedly requires the Department of Defense to explain its expenditures for chemical and biological research. The third are the National Institutes of Health guidelines intended to govern federally funded recombinant DNA research. Krimsky wrote in 1982 that these institutions were serving "to build public confidence."[13] Events since then have raised questions about this presumption.

In 1983, the cautious confidence expressed by observers like Zoch-linski and Krimsky began to yield to skepticism. Two important articles typified the new mood. The first, by Raymond Zilinskas, a molecular biologist and consultant to international organizations, offered a general accounting of potential problems with the new biology, including biological warfare.

Zilinskas discussed in the journal *Politics and the Life Sciences* several ways that recombinant DNA technology might be used in the service of the military. He mentioned enhancing the resistance of bacteria to antibiotic activity, and inducing bacteria to produce toxins and other "virulence factors" that they otherwise could not. Another approach would be to alter viruses against which antibodies now naturally present in the population would be ineffective. Before releasing such viruses, a vaccine could be developed and dispensed to the favored population.[14]

At the time of Zilinskas's writing, the incidence of AIDS (acquired immune deficiency syndrome) was rising dramatically. The disease, caused by a virus, seemed invariably fatal. Neither a person's own antibodies nor any known treatment appeared effective. The fear that AIDs prompted throughout the nation is a reminder of the horror that an uncontrolled biological agent could present to a vulnerable population.

Zilinskas's conjectures were not particularly novel, but they served as a catalyst for others to express their unease about military-related recombinant DNA work. Appended to his article were eight responses and commentaries that the editor of the journal had solicited. They came from scientists, social scientists, people in private enterprise and in government service. All endorsed Zilinskas's concerns about the use of biotechnology for military purposes, and agreed that standing treaty arrangements were not adequate to prevent illicit activities. The respondents' commentaries ranged from enthusiasm for a proposal by Zilinskas that the biological weapons treaty be altered to include verification procedures, to doubts that this would be effective.

Clifford Grobstein, a professor of biological science and public policy at the University of California in San Diego, despaired that "procedures for verification [are] now utterly lacking."[15] Sanford Lakoff, a political scientist at the same institution, minimized the importance of seeking verification procedures. They are unlikely to be accepted, he said, and would divert attention from "the most pressing need to extend the ban on biological agents or war to include toxic chemicals."[16] Despite such differences, respondents shared doubts that existing treaty arrangements would continue to prevent what they were intended to prevent—the development of biological weaponry. None of the commentators singled out any nation as more likely to be a transgressor than another. Their suspicions implicity were leveled as much at the United States as at the Soviet Union.

Shortly after Zilinskas's article and the accompanying commentaries were published, an article appeared in the *Bulletin of the Atomic Scientists* that detailed how much the United States was becoming involved with military contracts for genetic engineering research. Susan Wright, a historian of science at the University of Michigan, and Robert Sinsheimer, a biophysicist and chancellor at the University of California at Santa Cruz, expressed their concerns with less restraint than did Zilinskas and his commentators. Their worries were emblazoned in the article's lead: "A misuse of bioengineering technology for military purposes seems probable unless a reexamination of and a stronger commitment to biological weapons disarmament is forthcoming."[17]

The Wright/Sinsheimer article reviewed the reasons that concerns about recombinant DNA activity for military purposes had previously drawn little attention. The reasons rested largely with the perceived protection offered by the Biological Weapons Convention, and with statements of government officials that the United States had no plans to engage in such work. Such assurances had been fortified by the review conference of the parties to the Convention held in 1980. A briefing paper prepared by the Soviet Union, United States, and United Kingdom affirmed then that the development of fundamentally new dangerous microorganisms or toxins would be a task of "insurmountable complexity."[18]

Yet, as Wright and Sinsheimer pointed out, after 1980 the military became increasingly interested in genetic engineering research. By 1983, at least fourteen recombinant DNA research projects were underway under the sponsorship of the Department of Defense. They included the cloning of genes of various disease-causing organisms, introducing into bacteria the gene for a neural transmitter (acetylcholinesterase) that is attacked by nerve gas, and the development of detection and protective devices against biological agents. Some of the work was classified, although all, according to government spokesmen, was for defensive purposes.[19]

The authors said that the research thus far had not been designed to produce novel biological weapons, and was not technically in violation of the Biological Weapons Convention. But they were worried because "the kinds and extent of the Department's biological research—particularly the types contemplated as a response to threat of enemy use of genetic manipulation techniques—may raise doubts that such work will or can be completely in accord with the spirit of the Convention."[20]

Wright and Sinsheimer saw the biological weapons situation in 1983 as extremely tenuous, and likened it to the period in the late 1940s just before the start of the nuclear arms race. Because efforts to prevent that race failed, "we live in the deepening shadow of that failure." The authors issued a warning: "The use of the accumulated knowledge of biology for the construction of deadly pestilence is an ultimate perversion. Yet, unless we renounce the logic of protection and counterprotection, as exemplified in nuclear weaponry, it is a most likely development."[21]

Wright and Sinsheimer urged immediate action, including renunciation of secret biological research, and provisions for international inspection of biological laboratories wherever violations are suspected.[22] Their alarm was not shared by everyone. "Why rock the boat of an issue already settled for all practical purposes by a validated treaty which has worked so well to date?" wrote Martin Kaplan.[23] A microbiologist, Kaplan was secretary general of the Pugwash Conference on Science and World Affairs. He must have been surprised a few months after publishing his remarks, when the U.S. government made clear that it did not consider the issue settled. In April 1984, the Pentagon flatly charged that the "Soviet effort in biological warfare violates the Biological and Toxin Weapons Convention of 1972," and Secretary of Defense Weinberger called for keeping strong "our biological warfare deterrence."[24]

Other events during 1984 further fanned worries about a biological arms race. Contentiousness about the purported 1979 anthrax accident in Sverdlovsk had dissipated, and although the yellow rain debate was simmering, no new accusations had been made for more than a year. But now the government issued a roundhouse accusation against the Soviets in another area. Hitherto secret intelligence information alleged that the Soviets were engaged in a massive program to create biological weapons through recombinant DNA techniques. The accusation helped prompt more articles about biological warfare in 1984 than had appeared during the previous ten years.[25]

The Wall Street Journal Series

None was more important than a series of eight articles in the *Wall Street Journal* during April and May, entitled "Beyond 'Yellow Rain,' the Threat of Soviet Genetic Engineering."[26] The articles were written by William Kucewicz, an editorial writer for the newspaper, and they purported to show that the Soviet Union was engaged in a vigorous biological warfare program. They provided an overview of all the alleged Soviet activities that had previously been publicized, and many that had been secret. Because of their scope and the extraordinary amount of space provided them by an influential newspaper, the articles themselves were an event. They unvaryingly reflected the government's position that the Soviet's germ warfare activity was illegal, threatening, and growing. Addressing the articles became tantamount to addressing government policy.

A careful reading showed that the evidence offered in the series was sparse and indirect, as was documented in the *Bulletin of the Atomic Scientist* shortly afterward.[27] A critique of the *Journal* series highlights the weaknesses in the government's rationalization for expanding the United States biological weapons program.

The series mentions, early in the first installment, that the evidence "rests foremost on interviews with a number of former Soviet scientists now living in the U.S." Yet in the entire series only one such scientist who addresses the issue is named, Michael Zakharov. Zakharov had no first-hand knowledge, but heard from others that Soviet scientists were trying to develop biological weapons through recombinant DNA techniques. Other emigré scientists apparently agreed with Zakharov's story, but who they are is not revealed, since "they asked not to be identified" for fear of reprisal against friends and relatives. We never learn how many emigré scientists were interviewed, whether any were molecular biologists, or what relationship they had with the alleged biological warfare activities. If they did indeed provide the foundation for the *Journal's* sensational thesis, the reader is entitled to know more about them.

The only other named emigré who discusses the charges in the series is Mark Popovsky, a former science writer who left the Soviet Union in 1977. Popovsky tells of a meeting in 1974 at which Professor Yury A. Ovchinnikov, a vice president of the Soviet Academy of Sciences, announced that the Soviets would embark on a program to create bacteriological weapons through genetic engineering. While other (unnamed) emigrés agree that Ovchinnikov heads biological warfare research, at least one disputes the accuracy of Popovsky's version of the meeting.

Thus the only two emigré sources named in the *Journal's* series can hardly be considered unimpeachable witnesses. As for the unnamed scientists, were there two or twenty, and was their information based on rumor or fact? We are never told.

Kucewicz devotes the succeeding articles to particular issues that he says, make "an impressive case" that the Soviets are using genetic engineering to create battlefield bacteria. He cites the Soviet Union's past interest in biological weapons, the nature of certain scientific articles in recent years, the inability of an eminent microbiologist to emigrate, the alleged use of biological weapons in Afghanistan and Southeast Asia, and the anthrax epidemic in Sverdlovsk. That each of these issues is debatable he barely acknowledges.

The article dedicated to historical review is plainly irrelevant. Its centerpiece is a lengthy recapitulation of a report written in the late 1940s for U.S. intelligence, revealing that the Soviet Union was then involved in chemical and biological warfare preparations.[28] This evidently was meant to show that the Soviets have always been fond of bacterial weaponry and to explain the roots of today's purported program. It makes as much sense as quoting from a U.S. War Department report on the American biological warfare program written in 1946: "Work in this field, born of the necessity of war, cannot be ignored in time of peace; it must be continued."[29] Should such 1940s wisdom give rise to suspicion that today the United States is ignoring treaties that it subsequently signed? That seems to be the intended message about the Soviet Union.

Additional evidence of nefarious Soviet activity, Kucewicz believes, is found in the large number of articles in Soviet scientific literature on snake venoms and other neurotoxins. He acknowledges, however, that "Pentagon projects look similar to those in the Soviet open literature."[30] But this could mean that the Soviet Union is acting illegally, that the United States is, or that neither is.

In another non sequitur, we are told that the denial of an exit visa to Soviet microbiologist David Goldfarb helps confirm the existence of a genetic engineering weapons program.[31] After years of waiting, Goldfarb and his family received permission to emigrate to Israel early in 1984. Their visas were suspended when the KGB intervened, claiming that Goldfarb intended to take his collection of bacterial strains with him. While the KGB held that the material was of "national security importance," Goldfarb insisted that he never engaged in classified work. This leads the *Journal* to conclude that the Soviets show "particular sensitivity about microbiology" and supports suspicions that "Soviet Russia intends to use molecular genetics for biological warfare."[32]

In fact, Goldfarb was the first scientist of professional rank in *any* discipline to receive an exit visa in six years. If microbiology had become so patently connected to military activity, why were other microbiologists allowed to emigrate a few years ago, and why was

Goldfarb given an exit visa in the first place? Nan Griefer wrote in 1984 that many believe the Goldfarb case "had little to do with classified material, but reflected instead disagreement between the KGB and senior scientific circles who had gone over the KGB's head to get Goldfarb an exit visa."[33] About this nothing was mentioned in the *Journal*. The newspaper's proposition collapsed entirely in October 1986, when Goldfarb was allowed to leave the Soviet Union and to settle in the United States.

Articles in the series also discuss the "yellow rain" mycotoxins allegedly used by the Soviets or their surrogates in Afghanistan and Southeast Asia, and the 1979 anthrax epidemic in Sverdlovsk. In neither case is more than a nod offered to the fact that culpability and causes are in dispute. Rather, the reader is told that yellow rain is "the best-known demonstration of the active Soviet biochemical military program" and that without qualification the anthrax epidemic was caused by "an accident at a biological-weapons facility."[34]

Scientists still disagree, as discussed in Chapter 9, whether yellow rain was of natural or man-made origin. As for the anthrax outbreak in Sverdlovsk, the Soviet Union blamed it on tainted meat sold on the black market. The *Journal* opts for the U.S. government's conclusion that anthrax bacteria were released during an explosion at a biological weapons plant. Again the newspaper is selective with its evidence, ignoring the facts that anthrax is endemic in the Sverdlovsk areas and that an epidemic is always a potential danger there.

Elsewhere in the series, microbiologist Raymond A. Zilinskas is cited favorably when he agrees with the *Journal's* view that biological warfare has become technically more feasible.[35] Yet in the Sverdlovsk discussion Zilinskas's name is nowhere to be found. The newspaper's readers might have been interested to know that in 1983, Zilinskas assessed "all available information" and determined that the epidemic was most likely caused by "an infected animal . . . rendered into sausages and sold on the black market."[36]

The author of the series said that a secret U.S. intelligence report on the Sverdlovsk episode helped convince him of the validity of the government's version. Kucewicz cites the report as saying that after the epidemic began, Soviet epidemiologists arrived in Sverdlovsk, followed two weeks later by the defense and health ministers. "Their visits were not publicized," he writes.[37] Evidently this is supposed to suggest sinister activity. One might wonder why the defense minister took two weeks to arrive if there had been a military accident bearing such enormous implications.

All this is not to deny the possibility that the Soviets are trying to develop bacterial weapons by genetic engineering or that, as the

Journal declares, "the Soviet Union has never halted its biological weapons program."[38] But the move from possibility to probability requires stronger evidence than provided in the newspaper's series or by the Reagan administration.

For the *Journal*, the clinching argument that genetic engineering is "a natural and almost inevitable next step in the Soviet biochemical weapons program" is a passage in the 1983 edition of the Soviet *Military Encyclopedia*. Kucewicz is so impressed by the passage that he refers to it in three of the articles and offers identical quotations in two: "Achievements in biology and related sciences . . . have led to an increase in the effectiveness of biological agents as a means of conducting warfare."[39] Is this really an indication that the Soviets are engaged in biological weapons development? Raymond Zilinskas said almost the same thing in an American publication and, as mentioned, the *Journal* simply agreed with him.[40]

The thrust of the *Journal* series was to encourage more U.S. biological weapons activities, which could tempt this country to violate the 1972 Convention. The administration's statements, though not as blunt as those of the articles' author, essentially held the same thesis. From Secretary Weinberger's 1984 report:

> Soviet research efforts in the area of genetic engineering may also have a connection with their biological warfare program. There is an apparent effort on the part of the Soviets to transfer selected aspects of genetic engineering research to their biological warfare centers. For biological warfare purposes, genetic engineering could open a large number of possibilties. Normally harmless, non-disease producing organisms could be modified to become highly toxic or produce diseases for which an opponent has no known treatment or cure. Other agents, now considered too unstable for storage or biological warfare applications, could be changed sufficiently to be an effective agent.[41]

Despite the abundance of qualifiers, the tone of the remarks, like that of the *Journal* series, left little doubt about the administration's convictions. The final installment of the series concludes with an admonition that everyone should "come to grips with the Soviet genetic warfare program."[42] The Pentagon has made the same assumption. In 1984 it was engaged in or sponsoring 43 recombinant DNA projects, up from the 14 cited just one year earlier by Wright and Sinsheimer.[43]

Many American specialists who are familiar with Soviet scientific work question the Pentagon's rationale. "Ask any molecular biologist," says Dr. David Dubnau, a molecular biologist at the Public Health Research Institute in New York. "I've been to the Soviet Union five times and visited their laboratories." Dubnau rejects the possibility of greatly advanced work being done in secret. "You can't just do sophisticated work in one secret laboratory. You need a broad infrastructure in your universities and basic research labs which can inform the work being done in that particular laboratory." He concludes emphatically, "The Soviets don't have it."[44]

Meanwhile, Fort Detrick continues to sponsor increasing numbers of biological warfare projects that involve the development of vaccines and other defensive work. Even if these efforts remain defensive, American citizens have reason to worry. Among other activities, a return to outdoor testing over populated areas has never lost its appeal to some defense planners. As discussed in the next chapter, by the end of 1984 just such a proposal was made, and in 1986 field tests were underway.

Notes

1. Quoted in Sheldon Krimsky, *Genetic Alchemy: The Social History of the Recombinant DNA Controversy* (Cambridge: MIT Press, 1983), p. 31.

2. Bernard Dixon, "Biological Research (1)," *New Scientist* 60, no. 869 (October 25, 1973): 236.

3. Krimsky, *Genetic Alchemy*, p. 129.

4. Ibid., p. 131.

5. Ibid., p. 106.

6. Among several prominent volumes in the 1970s, the military issue is referred to in passing, or not at all. For example: June Goodfield, *Playing God: Genetic Engineering and the Manipulation of Life* (New York: Harper Colophon Books, 1977); Michael Rogers, *Biohazard* (New York: Alfred A. Knopf, 1977); Nicholas Wade, *The Ultimate Experiment: Man-Made Evolution* (New York: Walker & Co., 1977); Ted Howard and Jeremy Rifkin, *Who Should Play God?* (New York: Dell Publishing Co., 1978); John Lear, *Recombinant DNA: The Untold Story* (New York: Crown Publishers, 1978); Clifford Grobstein, *A Double Image of the Double Helix: The Recombinant-DNA Debate* (San Francisco: W. H. Freeman, 1979).

7. Liebe F. Cavalieri, *The Double-Edged Helix* (New York: Columbia University Press, 1981), p. 18.

8. Jonathan King, "Biological Weapons: Present and Future," paper presented at Symposium on Chemical and Biological Warfare: Past, Present and Future, at the Annual Meeting of the American Association for the Advancement of Science, 1982; idem, "The Threat of Biological Weapons," *Technology Review* (May/June 1982).

9. *Science* 209, no. 4462 (September 12, 1980): 1282.

10. *Science* 208, no. 4441 (April 18, 1980): 271.

11. Howard Zochlinski, "Inside Fort Detrick: Army DNA Researchers Try To Shed Bio-Warrior Image," *Genetic Engineering News*, September/October 1982, pp. 32–33.

12. Sheldon Krimsky, "Social Responsibility in an Age of Synthetic Biology," *Environment* 24, no. 6 (July/August 1982): 3–4.

13. Ibid., p. 4.

14. Raymond A. Zilinskas, "New Biotechnology: Potential Problems, Likely Promises," *Politics and the Life Sciences* 2, no. 1 (August 1983): 43–44.

15. Clifford Grobstein, "Who Is Janus?", *Politics and the Life Sciences* 2, no. 1 (August 1983): 56.

16. Sanford Lakoff, "Commentary on Zilinskas's Article," *Politics and the Life Sciences* 2, no. 1 (August 1983): 59.

17. Susan Wright and Robert Sinsheimer, "Recombinant DNA and Biological Warfare," *Bulletin of the Atomic Scientists* 39, no. 9 (November 1983): 20.

18. Ibid., p. 21.

19. Ibid., p. 22.

20. Ibid., p. 23.

21. Ibid.

22. Ibid., p. 26.

23. Martin M. Kaplan, "Another View," *Bulletin of the Atomic Scientists* 39, no. 9 (November 1983): 27.

24. U.S. Department of Defense. *Soviet Military Power, 1984* (Washington, D.C.: Government Printing Office, 1984), p. 73; *New York Times*, April 11, 1984, p. A-21.

25. In 1984, beside many news accounts about particular issues like yellow rain (see Chapter 9) or the Dugway issue (see Chapter 11), feature stories on the general subject abounded. An eight-article series, "Beyond 'Yellow Rain,' the Threat of Soviet Genetic Engineering," appeared in the *Wall Street Journal* (see note 26 for dates), and syndicated columns on the subject by Jack Anderson were published in hundreds of newspapers (for example, "Soviets Push Biological-Weapons Work," *Washington Post*, December 4, 1984, p. B-15). See also John Hubner, "The Hidden Arms Race," *West* (Sunday Magazine of the *San Jose Mercury News*), April 15, 1984; Robert Ruttman, " 'Strictly Anti-Human' Chemical and Biological Warfare," *Science for the People* 16, no. 3 (May/June 1984); Richard Asinoff, "Averting Genetic Warfare," *Environmental Action*, June 1984; R. Jeffrey Smith, "The Dark Side of Biotechnology," *Science* 224, no. 4654 (June 15, 1984); "Chemical and Bacteriological Weapons in the 1980s," *The Lancet*, July 21, 1984; Joseph D. Douglass, Jr., and H. Richard Lukens, "The Expanding Arena of Chemical-Biological Warfare," *Strategic Review*, Fall 1984; and Jonathan B. Tucker, "Gene Wars," *Foreign Policy* 57 (Winter 1984–85).

26. William Kucewicz, "Beyond 'Yellow Rain,' the Threat of Soviet Genetic Engineering" (*Wall Street Journal*) articles appeared on April 23, 25, and 27; May 1, 3, 8, 10, and 18, 1984.

27. Leonard A. Cole, "Yellow Rain or Yellow Journalism?" *Bulletin of the Atomic Scientists* 40, no. 7 (August/September 1984). Much of the remaining discussion in this chapter is derived from the article.

28. Kucewicz, May 10, 1984, p. 34.

29. "Report to the Secretary of War by George W. Merck, Special Consultant for Biological Warfare" (January 3, 1946), in U.S. Congress: Senate Hearings before the Subcommittee on Health and Scientific Research of the Committee on Human Resources, *Biological Testing Involving Human Subjects by the Department of Defense, 1977*, March 8 and May 23, 1977 (Washington, D.C.: Government Printing Office, 1977), p. 71.

30. Kucewicz, May 18, 1984, p. 26.

31. Kucewicz, May 8, 1984, p. 34.

32. Ibid.

33. Nan Greifer, *Jews in the Soviet Union* (London: National Council for Soviet Jewry of the United Kingdom and Ireland, 1984).

34. Kucewicz, April 23, 1984, p. 30; May 3, 1983, p. 28.

35. Kucewicz, May 18, 1984, p. 26.

36. Raymond A. Zilinskas, "Anthrax in Sverdlovsk?" *Bulletin of the Atomic Scientists* 39, no. 6 (June/July 1983): 26.

37. Kucewicz, May 3, 1984, p. 28.

38. Ibid., p. 34.

39. Kucewicz, April 23, 1984, p. 30; April 27, 1984, p. 28; and May 18, 1984, p. 26.

40. The passage by Zilinskas cited in the *Journal* states that in 1969, "The military could see no situation where biological warfare could be of practical use in conflicts, and therefore it was easy to give up. However, the situation has changed drastically since 1969. New techniques can now be employed to overcome previously existing technical limitations to biological warfare" (Kucewicz, May 18, 1984, p. 26).

41. *Soviet Military Power, 1984*, p. 73.

42. Kucewicz, May 18, 1984, p. 26.

43. Ibid.

44. Interview, March 27, 1985.

11

Return to Testing

Field Experiments, the Dugway Issue,
and Ethical Questions

Recommendations to Test

THE ADMINISTRATION'S VIEW of Soviet perfidy in the areas of
biological and chemical warfare has led to increased concerns
about the nation's vulnerability and defenses. In line with these
concerns, the army contracted with the National Academy of Sciences
to assess U.S. ability to detect chemical and biological agents. The
Academy's Board on Army Science and Technology established a
committee of twelve scientists to study the issue, and in August 1984
the committee issued a 110-page report, *Assessment of Chemical and
Biological Sensor Technologies.*

The report reviews the characteristics of several known chemical,
biological, and toxin agents, and lists "some infectious agents of
potential BW concern." Among the biologicals, the list includes various viruses, rickettsiae, bacteria, fungi, and protozoa. They account
for twenty-four agents of disease, most of which have been considered biological warfare threats since the United States became interested in the issue during World War II. The report indicates that
influenza, smallpox, typhus, anthrax, brucellosis, cholera, plague, and
the like remain no less a worry to biological warfare planners today
than forty years ago.

As was true forty years ago, there is still no way to detect, let alone
defend against, a surprise attack with such weaponry. With scarcely
an acknowledgement that extensive vulnerability testing had been
conducted for decades, the committee simply says that research
involving "the detection of biological agents" has been minimal.[1] The
implied message is that the hundreds of previous vulnerability tests
have been useless.

The largest section of the report reviews a panoply of current and potential sensing techniques that the committee thinks might be applicable to chemical and biological detection devices. They include microsensors, immunoassays, gene probes, biochips, and other exotic technologies. Whether any of these could be contrived to detect a biological warfare attack remains problematic.

The state-of-the-art review is followed by a discussion of constraints on sensor development. In this section, the report criticizes "battlefield integration plans" that do not seek information about chemical and biological warfare. Commanders have access to sensors like radar and acoustic and infrared devices, but nothing that provides "detailed information on chemical and biological agents if they are used in an attack."[2] Other constraints are mentioned, such as the limited funding available for developing detection devices and the "hundreds of steps" and "many years" required for their development. The report then notes with disapproval inhibitions on open-air testing.[3] This observation, casually included among the constraints, takes on ominous proportions by the end of the report.

The final section, titled "Conclusions and Recommendations," summarizes the material that had been discussed in the earlier portions and suggests further exploration. For detection of chemicals, various sensor technologies are mentioned, such as mass spectroscopy, microsensor technologies, and semipermeable membranes. The recommendation is simply that "chemical sensors should be developed in the areas outlined above."[4]

Biological agents seem more fearsome to the committee. It concludes that "the diversity of biologically derived chemical weapons and biological agents, as well as their ability to cause immediate and delayed casualties makes them prime candidates for incorporation in an enemy's chemical warfare capability." The recommendation: "The overall effort to detect and identify biological agents and toxins should be accelerated, with concentration in those areas involving biotechnology".[5]

The report then reviews the need to develop better sensing ability of "meterological variables" and of remote "clouds or contaminated areas."[6] In the end, the committee's conclusions and recommendations overshadow what had been discussed in the earlier sections. If there had been any doubt previously, if the committee's interest in open air vulnerability testing had seemed circumspect, the final sentences were unambiguous:

> Conclusion At this time, chemical detection devices are not being field tested. There are insufficient enclosures suitable for testing equip-

ment with actual agents under field conditions. Laboratory testing of actual agents is not deemed adequate to represent properly field tests of the detectors under operational conditions.

Recommendation The problem of inadequate testing of detection devices, particularly those for actual agents, should be addressed.

Conclusion There is a critical need for realistic, nontoxic simulants for both field testing and training exercises. Current models are inadequate to replace field tests to define the characteristics of detectors.

Recommendation Realistic, nontoxic simulants for both field testing and training be developed early.[7]

Except for the appendices, these were the closing words of the committee's report. "Realistic, nontoxic simulants"—the same kind of words the army used in the past and continues to use, to describe zinc cadmium sulfide, *Serratia marcescens, Bacillus subtilis,* and the other agents that were sprayed in earlier tests over populated areas.

Nowhere in the report is there an indication that testing should be confined to unpopulated areas, nor is the question of exposing unsuspecting citizens mentioned. After the report was issued, two scientists who served on the committee were asked about the report's omission concerning the exposed population. Neither could recall any discussions about the subject during committee deliberations.[8] One member, Dr. F. James Primus, an immunologist at the University of Medicine and Dentistry of New Jersey, doubted that the committee intended that testing be conducted in heavily populated areas, although "field tests presumably would be done where there are people." Indeed, the report's admonition that "nontoxic" biological and chemical simulants be used implies an understanding that people would be exposed.

Dr. Primus said that "we just don't have any sensors for biological agents." He is especially worried that genetic engineering techniques could lead to "new biological agents that we can't design sensors to detect." With chemicals, he continued, "we can develop mass spectrometers, but in the biological area we just don't know what to do." Dr. Primus's concern, like the committee's, was principally with "the feeling that the Russians are developing toxic capabilities," and not where open air testing might take place.

Although the army had contracted to obtain the information contained in the committee's report, army spokesmen remained vague about what they intended to do with it. During an interview in May 1985, Colonel Robert Orton, head of the army's nuclear-biological-chemical defense division, said the army has "taken no decision at all to go back into the business of open air testing." When asked about the Army Science and Technology committee's recommendation to resume field testing, he said that "the report is incorporated and used as a source document as we develop all our programs across the board. We evaluate it among other studies and other needs."[9]

Shortly after these remarks were made, impetus from another direction pointed to the resumption of open air testing. A Chemical Warfare Review Commission that had been appointed by the president earlier in the year issued its conclusions in June 1985. The eight-member commission, chaired by former Undersecretary of State Walter J. Stoessel, was asked to assess the nation's chemical warfare needs. Although "the realm of biological weapons" was not part of its charter, the commission included the subject because "modern biochemistry . . . has blurred the line between the chemical and the biological."[10]

The Stoessel commission's report echoed the administration's certitude that the Soviets had violated the Biological Weapons Convention. Ignoring doubts expressed by scientists and other former government officials, the commissioners deplored "the magnitude of the Soviet chemical warfare effort, and, even more, Soviet biological warfare advances."[11]

The commissioners accused the Defense Department of not having "an adequate grasp of the biological-warfare threat," and called for devoting "much more resources and talent" to address the subject.[12] What should be done? Among the commission's suggestions: conduct open air testing "in a realistic setting."[13] The commission aimed its proposal to test at the need to develop shelters and detection equipment. The term "realistic setting," however, evokes images of past tests over populated areas—those areas of vulnerability that army officials previously said might require additional testing.

By 1986 the army had moved further in that direction. A report in May by the Defense Department to the House Appropriations Committee about the biological defense program revealed that open air testing was underway at the Dugway Proving Ground in Utah. Beside "developing and validating" new simulants, the army acknowledged that it was using Bacillus subtilis and Serratia marcescens in outdoor tests there, the same bacteria it had used in previous years across the country.[14] The report endorsed spraying with these bacteria because "they offer several advantages." Unlike more potent organisms that actually would be used as biological weapons, these simulants "reduce the hazards to people and the environment." Their use, accordingly, "reduces safety procedure and monitoring requirements, which saves manpower and equipment expenses."[15]

The army evidently feels no greater need now than in the past to monitor the condition of people exposed to these bacteria. None of the questions about health, safety, or ethics that emerged in the aftermath of the earlier tests appear in the 1986 report. The army's inattention to these issues is reminiscent of its attitude about its tests over cities in the 1950s and 1960s. It continues to assume that spraying these organisms around people will not cause problems. As discussed in previous chapters, the assumption is gratuitous.

The report was presented to the appropriations committee to justify Pentagon requests for more money for the biological defense program. It reiterated the official position that the Soviets were violating the 1972 Biological Weapons Convention and that the United States now faces a "serious biological warfare threat."[18] Yet in May 1986, the month that the report was issued, the man who headed the U.S. negotiating team that led to the signing of the 1972 Convention offered a different view.

James Leonard, now retired from the Foreign Service, spoke to the subject at a panel sponsored by the American Association for the Advancement of Science. Joining the skepticism voiced by many scientists and scholars, he concluded that "there is no convincing evidence that the Soviets have violated the Biological Weapons Convention or the Geneva Protocol." Regarding the yellow rain charges, he continued, "this government has acted shamefully. We have made charges that we cannot substantiate."[17]

Not a word about such skepticism appeared in the army's 1986 report. Nor were locations for future open air tests specified, who would be exposed, how often, for what duration, or under what conditions.

How the army will incorporate into its open air test program the proposals to test under realistic conditions may only be surmised. But based on past performance there is reason for concern. As officials who had been in charge of previous tests in San Francisco, Washington, D. C., the New York City subways, and other cities acknowledged during the Nevin trial in 1981, these locations were chosen precisely because the army wanted to simulate realistic conditions.

"Don't say, 'Why didn't you do this in some salt mine'" General William Creasy had testified during the Nevin trial. "Because if you want to test the B. W. agent, the B. W. agent is designed to work against people. You have to test them in the kind of place where people live and work."[18]

Field Testing with Genetically Altered Organisms

Another series of events with implications for open air testing was prompted by changes in the National Institutes of Health (NIH) guidelines on recombinant DNA research. In 1982, the guidelines were relaxed to allow experiments involving the release of genetically altered organisms into the environment, although each experiment would have to be approved by the NIH.

The following year, the NIH approved requests by several institutions to conduct open air tests with organisms containing recombined DNA. Public interest organizations, including the Foundation on Economic Trends, Environmental Action, and Environmental Task Force, joined in a federal suit to prohibit the carrying out of such tests. The principal spokesman for the group, Jeremy Rifkin, head of the Foundation on Economic Trends, is a long-standing opponent of all recombinant DNA research.

The focus of the suit dealt with a proposed experiment by University of California scientists with bacteria called *Pseudomonas syringae*. At near-freezing temperatures, these bacteria form particles around which ice crystalizes. Since the bacteria are common in the environment, they induce frost damage to many agricultural crops. The California scientists wanted to spray a potato patch with *Pseudomonas syringae* that had been genetically altered to eliminate their frost-making capability. The scientists hoped that the modified bacteria would displace their naturally occurring counterparts and reduce damage from frost.

The suit argued that the consequences of such an experiment could not be foreseen:

> Experiments involving recombinant DNA organisms released into the environment present four risk components: First, there is the possibility that the organism will survive in the environment; second, that it will grow in that environment; third, that it will displace, compete with, and disrupt other organisms and the ecosystem; and fourth, that it will be harmful.[19]

The suit held further that the NIH's revised guidelines were inappropriate because they were prepared without an environmental impact statement or an environmental assessment. In consequence, it called for the prohibition of this type of research.[20]

Despite arguments by the University of California scientists that the experiment posed no environmental threat, in May 1984 Judge John J. Sirica blocked the project. He held that an overall environmental impact statement about outdoor testing should be prepared, and suggested that a case-by-case approach as presently provided by NIH policy was inadequate.[21]

The following month the NIH's advisory committee on recombinant DNA disregarded Judge Sirica's admonition and approved additional proposals for outdoor testing by two private companies. (Although the guidelines technically apply only to institutions receiving federal funds, private companies have acceded to them as well.) One of the approved projects, requested by a company called Advanced Genetic Sciences, would involve a field test with the same kind of genetically altered *Pseudomonas syringae* as in the California proposal, but sprayed on strawberry plants rather than potatoes.[22]

Rifkin's group quickly returned to court. It sought not only to prevent the experiment, but to obtain a court order granting NIH authority over all genetic outdoor experiments, whether by privately or federally funded institutions. The NIH opposed expansion of its own authority.

Meanwhile, in October 1984, the Environmental Protection Agency (EPA) entered the regulatory controversy. It issued its first policy statement regarding genetically engineered substances. The EPA's involvement was prompted by the efforts of companies to test pesticides that were manufactured through recombinant DNA techniques. Unlike for conventional pesticides, producers would have to give notice to the agency before testing outdoors with genetically engineered substances. Microorganisms would be treated differently, according to the statement, because chemicals have "no independent mobility and reproductive capability; therefore their potential for causing adverse effects outside the project area is extremely limited."[23]

In 1985, the EPA approved two field test proposals with genetically altered organisms, including the one by Advanced Genetic Sciences that had previously received the support of the NIH advisory committee. Rifkin's group again filed suit and the tests were postponed. But on April 24, 1987, after a California court rejected further delays, Advanced Genetic Sciences conducted the first outdoor experiment with genetically engineered bacteria. The company's technicians, clad from head to foot in protective outfits according to federal regulation, sprayed bacteria over a patch of 2,500 strawberry plants in California's Central Valley. The company continued to maintain that its open air experiment was harmless.[24]

The implications of the issue for outdoor testing by the army are twofold. One is symbolic, the other substantive. Expanding the permissible limits of open air experimentation with microorganisms will strengthen the army's sense of legitimacy about its testing program. Approval of open air tests with genetically modified organisms can only encourage the notion that biological warfare vulnerability testing is safe and, in the army's view, no less important than any other program.

Second, the quest for an ideal simulant for outdoor testing may encourage the army to turn to recombinant DNA technology. What better simulant can there be of *Bacillus anthracis*, for example, than the bacillus itself, slightly altered to eliminate its ability to cause anthrax? Those, like the committee of the Army Science and Technology Board, who believe that a realistic, nontoxic simulant should be used in open air tests might well consider this an ideal simulant agent.

Dr. David Swift, a professor of environmental health sciences at Johns Hopkins University, and a member of the committee, was asked about the idea. He said that he was not an expert on recombinant DNA, but that the proposition seemed to have "interesting possibilities." Similarly, Dr. F. James Primus, another committee member, thought that if pathogenicity were genetically eliminated, an organism could be considered a "harmless simulant."[25]

Saul Hormats, a retired director of development for the Army Chemical Corps, once closely associated with the biological warfare program, holds a different view.

> It's the most stupid damn thing I ever heard. You don't just change bacteria like pulling the radio out of a car and the car runs around with no radio. You change a lot of other things as well. You can't assume that all the other characteristics are unchanged. Bugs don't work that way. You change it entirely—your immune responses will be different; you couldn't detect it on your alarms; everything would be changed. You can't throw out one part of a living organism and not change other parts as well.[26]

In the midst of the recombinant DNA–field testing controversy, a Pentagon official alluded to the possibility of more army open air tests. At a symposium on Biological Research and Military Policy sponsored by the American Association for the Advancement of Science in May 1984, Thomas Dashiell, director of environmental and life sciences in the Office of the Secretary of Defense, was asked about resumed testing with microorganisms and chemicals over populated areas. "I would hesitate to guess on whether there will be a resumption or not," said Dashiell, who was once assistant scientific director at Fort Detrick. He tried to reassure his audience by explaining that "any open air testing at this point in time requires the completion of a complete and detailed environmental impact statement which is made public. We hold public hearings on all of those."[27]

Dashiell was referring to the requirements of the National Environmental Policy Act of 1969 concerning any federal action that would significantly affect the environment. Yet before the end of the year the army was treating the biological weapons issue in a way that raised questions about the army's forthrightness.

The Dugway Issue

Before Congress adjourned in August 1984, an acting assistant secretary of the army sent a note to the House and Senate appropriations committees requesting a routine reallocation of $66 million. The funds were to be taken from existing programs and used for several apparently minor projects. The list included new military housing in Europe, a parking garage in upstate New York, and a physical fitness center in Pennsylvania. Tucked among such items was an aerosol test facility in Utah.[28]

The request was reviewed by the chairmen and ranking minority members of the subcommittees on military construction. As is customary, upon their assent the reallocation was authorized. Two months later, Senator James Sasser, the ranking minority member on the Senate subcommittee and one of the four members who signaled assent, reversed his position. In a letter to Secretary of Defense Casper Weinberger, he explained that after reviewing the planned expansion of the test facility at Dugway Proving Ground in Utah, he determined that it could be used "to test offensive biological and toxin weapons, a capability which is prohibited by a 1972 Treaty."[29]

The heart of the facility, according to an army information paper sent to Congress soon afterward, would be a steel chamber in which "aerosol studies of extremely hazardous viruses and other biomaterials" would take place. The facility presumably would not be involved with open air testing, but would be used to test military equipment and "provide laboratory support for biothreat studies." The paper also explained that this was only part of a "modernization" program for Dugway Proving Ground, which over the next five years would cost more than $300 million.[30]

Despite Pentagon assurances that the new test facility would not violate the treaty, Sasser remained skeptical. On December 6th, the other four members of the Senate subcommittee decided to approve the $8.4 million reprogramming request for the project over Sasser's objection. Unknown to the public, however, the chairman of the Senate Appropriations Committee, Mark Hatfield, had been working "to do all we could" to delay approval of the project. He wrote a letter expressing his objections to the subcommittee chairman, Mack Mattingly, because "I wanted to be on record as opposing the chemical and biological modernization effort."[31]

Hatfield's letter, whose contents were not previously made public, indicates concern about "a host of issues which are raised by the Dugway modernization plans, particularly in the biological research area." Among them he lists "transportation and storage of toxins, use of animals and potentially humans for research, security against terrorism, coordination with our allies, and compliance with existing environmental law and international treaty agreements. . . . All these potential problems," he went on to say, "should be addressed *before* Congress approves funding for project construction." The word "before" is underlined in the letter.

Hatfield's letter criticizes the manner used by the army to try to expand its biological warfare facilities, calling the request "sufficiently controversial as to warrant more rigorous scrutiny than is associated with a routine 'reprogramming.' " An aide to Senator Hatfield later emphasized that the senator would be "monitoring the [issue] very carefully."

Meanwhile, Jeremy Rifkin's Foundation on Economic Trends filed a suit in federal court to stop the project. Rifkin and his group were already notorious for bringing genetic engineers to court to prevent the introduction of genetically altered bacteria into the environment. The suit against the army, which was joined by retired Admiral Gene LaRocque, the director of the Center for Defense Information, focused on concerns that toxic material might escape from the laboratory.[32] It contended that the project would impose risks to the health of people in the area, and that the Department of Defense had "wantonly disregarded the federal statute governing environmental risk assessment."

In response to the suit, the Defense Department suspended the start of construction and issued an environmental assessment of the project. The assessment maintained that all toxic materials would be contained within the new facility and would therefore have no effect on the environment. Rifkin and his organization quickly filed for an injunction to halt further development of the project, pending the army's writing a formal environmental impact statement. By law, preparing such a statement requires public hearings and consideration of alternatives.

On May 31, 1985, Federal District Court Judge Joyce Hens Green ruled in favor of the plaintiffs, and enjoined the army from "taking further action to advance the construction of the proposed" facility. She found the risks of building the aerosol test laboratory, less than 90 miles from Salt Lake City, to be "serious and far-reaching." She criticized not only the superficiality of the army's environmental assessment, but the army's cavalier approach to several related issues. From Judge Green's ruling:

An environmental assessment must offer something more than a "checklist" of assurances and alternatives. It must indicate, in some fashion, that the agency has taken a searching, realistic look at the potential hazards and, with reasoned thought and analysis, candidly and methodically addressed these concerns.

Measured against these standards, the Environmental Assessment published by the Army is clearly inadequate. . . . No mention is made of the unique geographical characteristics of the surrounding area, the degree to which the action is likely to be controversial, the extent to which the possible effects on the human environment are likely to be unknown, the long- and short-term effects on the local region and "on society as a whole," the degree to which the action may adversely affect an endangered or threatened species, and the possibility, if any, that the action may threaten a violation of federal, state, or local laws or requirements imposed "for the protection of the environment."[33]

The comprehensiveness of the judge's critique left the army little hope of reversing the decision on appeal, and construction of the testing facility was postponed. The army later indicated its intention to complete an environmental impact statement sometime in 1988.

The series of events should concern anyone worried about unwittingly breathing in army germs during open air tests. The manner in which the army sought to implement its project—without formal votes, hearings, or debates—is disturbing. There seemed to be an effort to avoid deliberate consideration of "an unprecedented expansion of the army's biological weapons research program," in the words of an article in *Science* magazine.[34] Only when threatened with legal action did the army agree to an environmental assessment. This is all the more troubling in view of Dashiell's assurances a few months earlier, when he said that tests that might expose people to biological agents would be preceded by an environmental impact statement and public hearings. When asked about this after the Dugway issue erupted, Dashiell repeated the army's contention that the project would not affect the environment and that no statement was necessary.

Meanwhile, according to an aide to Senator Sasser, the senator remained concerned about how the army sought funding for the laboratory, "despite the assurances that have been given." An aide to Senator Hatfield was more blunt: "If you put the pieces together you see a drift toward wanting to test on human beings."[35]

In December 1984, Governor Scott Matheson of Utah had asked his attorney general to consider joining the Rifkin suit on behalf of the state. Matheson left office at the end of the year and no action was taken, but "I still feel just as strongly about it," he says. Matheson recalls his frustration in previous years when he sought information about radiation hazards from atomic tests in his state. "The only information we have now about this new Dugway facility is what the military has voluntarily released," he continues, "and this is never satisfactory to me, from personal experience."[36] Doubt that the army would inform the public before spraying it with bacteria is only reinforced by the way the army has handled the Dugway episode.

Ironically, several scientists who oppose the Dugway project implicitly lend support to open air spraying. Concerned about the use of toxic agents, they endorse the plea in Rifkin's suit that simulants be used as an alternative. Roy Curtiss, a molecular biologist and chairman of the biology department at Washington University, says that instead of pathogenic organisms, "one can easily choose nonpathogenic or avirulent agents with the same size and molecular properties."[37]

Other scientists have written memoranda to this effect in behalf of the Rifkin suit. When asked if this might not lend support to the army's argument that spraying populated areas with simulants is harmless, some were taken aback. "I never thought of that," said Richard Goldstein, professor of infectious diseases at the Boston University School of Medicine. "I guess one can take anything out of context and distort it," he added. Dr. David Dubnau agreed that this could be "a very important concern." He said he was troubled by it because he "would be very much opposed to their using simulants outside of this closed facility."[38]

Thus, however unintentionally, critics of the army's proposed facility at Dugway may be seen as promoting the idea that spraying "nontoxic" agents would be safe—which has been the army's contention all along. Yet as Dr. George Connell of the Centers for Disease Control testified at the Senate hearings in 1977, "there is no such thing as a microorganism that cannot cause trouble." Speaking of the supposedly harmless bacteria used in the germ warfare tests, he emphasized that "if you get the right concentration at the right place, at the right time, and in the right person, something is going to happen."[39]

Dr. Richard Goldstein is even less forgiving: "You give me any normally 'nonpathogenic' microbe and under certain conditions it can be pathogenic. Any simulant is potentially a pathogen. I don't care what microbe it is." He concludes, "Once one talks about the release of microorganisms, there is no such thing as safety."

Nevertheless, the army's long-standing position, which was endorsed in the recent reports urging more field tests, and inadvertently by scientists who have criticized the Dugway project, is that "nontoxic" simulants are harmless and may be used over populated areas.

Ethical Implications

Apart from questions of safety, the right of citizens not to be unsuspecting guinea pigs should be at issue. Yet here too protection falls through the cracks of institutional safeguards. The National Research Act of 1974 was enacted after the disclosure two years earlier of research that had been going on in Tuskegee, Alabama. For forty years, U.S. Public Health Service doctors there ostensibly had been treating syphilitic black men, but in fact were dispensing placebos so they could study the course of the disease. The 1974 Act reflected concern about the Tuskegee research and about the rights and welfare of human experimental subjects in general. It provided that every federal agency that engages in research involving human subjects have a review board that must approve each project. Informed consent is supposed to be a central consideration in such reviews.

On the surface, protection of an unsuspecting public from army germs would seem assured insofar as targeted citizens should be informed and give consent. "Not necessarily," says Alexander Capron, who was executive director of the President's commission on bioethics before it went out of existence in 1983. Now a professor of law at the University of Southern California, Capron says the army's definition of research is different from what some people might wish. "If they develop a new battle plan or a new weapon, the army does not regard that as coming under the regulations on human experimentation."[40] Battlefield exercises, especially with unloaded or otherwise harmless weapons, would not be considered research on humans.

When asked about this, Thomas Dashiell of the Office of the Secretary of Defense explains that before any such weapons would be used in training exercises, "we do a whole series of tests to insure that they meet military requirements, and that they're not harmful from the occupational, safety and health aspects." He sees "no problem at all" in using such weaponry, and this would have nothing to do with human subject research.

A second complication, according to Capron, involves whether people who are sprayed during a germ warfare test should be considered experimental subjects. "To me it would be pretty clear that they are," he says, "but to others, when you deal with widely dispersed testing, there may be some question as to who are the subjects." A

Pentagon official involved in interpreting the defense department's human-subject regulations concurs that people exposed in open air tests "would not in fact be experimental subjects."[41]

Thus, according to the army's position that its test bacteria are harmless, and that exposed citizens may not be viewed as experimental subjects, spraying could be taking place and no one would know. There are many reasons to worry about the Pentagon's resurgent biological warfare program, including whether it is in response to a real or imagined Soviet provocation. But one issue is clear: present policy does not adequately protect the rights and safety of citizens who may be exposed during vulnerability tests.

Notes

1. *Assessment of Chemical and Biological Sensor Technologies*, A Report by the Committee on Chemical and Biological Sensor Technologies, Board on Army Science and Technology, National Research Council of the National Academy of Sciences (Washington, D. C.: National Academy Press, 1984), p. 6.

2. Ibid., p. 49.

3. Ibid., pp. 52, 56–57.

4. Ibid., pp. 61–62.

5. Ibid., p. 62.

6. Ibid., pp. 66–68.

7. Ibid., p. 70.

8. Interviews with Dr. David L. Swift and Dr. F. James Primus, January 17, 1985.

9. Interview, May 25, 1985.

10. *Report of the Chemical Warfare Review Commission* (Washington, D. C.: Government Printing Office, June 1985), p. 69. The eight members were nationally prominent figures, but few had previous experience with biological or chemical warfare matters. Beside Walter Stoessel, they included Philip Bakes, president of Continental Airlines; Zbigniew Brzezinski, former assistant to the president for National Security Affairs; Richard Cavazos, retired army general; Barber Conable, former Congressman; John Erlenborn, former Congressman; Alexander Haig, former general and Secretary of State; John Kester, attorney.

11. Ibid., p. 67.

12. Ibid., p. 71.

13. Ibid., p. 65.

14. U.S. Department of Defense. "Biological Defense Program," Report to the Committee on Appropriations, House of Representatives, Washington, D. C., May 1986, chap. 1, p. 11; chap. 9, p. 2 (mimeographed).

15. Ibid., chap. 4, p. 1.

16. Ibid., Executive Summary, p. 1.

17. Panel on Strengthening the Prohibition Against Biological Warfare, Annual Meeting of the American Association for the Advancement of Science, May 27, 1986. Similar remarks appeared in James Leonard, "Re-

viewing the Biological Weapons Convention," *Issues in Science and Technology* 3, no. 1. (Fall 1986): 12–13.

18. Trial transcript, *Mabel Nevin, et al., Plaintiffs, vs. United States of America, Defendant*, before Judge Samuel Conti, United States District Court, Northern District of California, No. C 78–1713 SC, March 16–March 31, 1981, p. 625.

19. *Foundation on Economic Trends, et al., Plaintiffs, vs. Margaret Heckler, et al., Defendants*, Civil Action No. 83–2714, United States District Court for the District of Columbia, September 14, 1983, p. 15.

20. Ibid., pp. 17–20.

21. *New York Times*, May 25, 1984, p. A–22.

22. Harold M. Schmeck, Jr., "Panel Approves the Release of Genes Altered by Science," *New York Times*, June 2, 1984, p. 8.

23. Philip Shabecoff, "E. P. A. Sets Rules for Genetically Altered Pesticide," *New York Times*, October 5, 1984, p. A–13.

24. Keith Schneider, "Gene-Altered Bacteria Released in a Historic Experiment Outdoors," *New York Times*, April 25, 1987, p. 1. See also Marjorie Sun, "EPA Approves Field Test of Altered Microbes," *Science* 230, no. 4729 (November 29, 1985): 1015–16. As described in Sun's article, federal jurisdiction and standards concerning recombinant DNA activities remain unclear.

25. Interview, January 17, 1985.

26. Interview, September 13, 1985.

27. Transcript of Symposium on Biological Research and Military Power, Annual Meeting of the American Association for the Advancement of Science, Washington, D. C., May 26, 1984.

28. R. Jeffrey Smith, "New Army Biowarfare Lab Raises Concerns," *Science* 226, no. 4679 (December 7, 1984): 1176–78.

29. Letter from Senator James Sasser to Secretary of Defense Caspar W. Weinberger, October 31, 1984.

30. Information Paper to Congress from the Department of the Army, "Modernization of Dugway Proving Ground," DAMA-PPM-T, November 8, 1984 (mimeographed).

31. During a telephone conversation on May 23, 1985, Senator Mark Hatfield's press secretary read to me portions of the senator's previously undisclosed letter to Senator Mack Mattingly, written in December 1984.

32. Complaint for Declaratory and Injunctive Relief, *Foundation on Economic Trends, et al., Plaintiffs, vs. Caspar W. Weinberger, et al., Defendants*, Civil Action No. 84–3452, United States District Court for the District of Columbia, November 21, 1984.

33. Memorandum Opinion and Order by Judge Joyce Hens Green, re *Foundation on Economic Trends, et al., Plaintiffs, vs. Caspar W. Weinberger, et al., Defendants*, Civil Action No. 84–3542, United States District Court for the District of Columbia, May 31, 1985.

34. Smith, "New Army Biowarfare Lab," p. 1176.

35. Conversations with Senator Sasser's and Senator Hatfield's aides were held in March, April, and May 1985.

36. Interview with former Governor Scott M. Matheson, March 28, 1985.

37. Quoted in Smith, "New Army Biowarfare Lab," p. 1177.

38. Interviews with Dr. Richard Goldstein and Dr. David Dubnau, March

27, 1985. Memoranda in support of Rifkin's suit were filed by Dr. Richard P. Novick, Director of the Public Health Research Institute; Dr. David A. Dubnau, Department of Biology, Public Health Research Institute; Dr. Liebe F. Cavalieri, Professor of Biochemistry, Cornell Medical College; Dr. David Ozonoff, Chief of Environmental Health Section, Boston University School of Public Health; Dr. Robert L. Sinsheimer, Chancellor, University of California—Santa Cruz.

39. U.S. Congress: Senate Hearings before the Subcommittee on Health and Scientific Research of the Committee on Human Resources, *Biological Testing Involving Human Subjects by the Department of Defense, 1977*, March 8 and May 23, 1977 (Washington, D. C.: Government Printing Office, 1977), p. 270.

40. Quotations are from an interview on June 2, 1982, reiterated in conversations in February 1985.

41. Interview, February 13, 1985. Public Law No. 91–121, enacted in November 1969, requires the defense department to give advanced notice to congressional and local officials about experiments "involving the use of human subjects for the testing of chemical or biological agents." If the army believes that people exposed to bacteria in open air tests are not experimental subjects, it is not likely to announce its tests, either before or after they are conducted.

12

Worries and Ambiguities

READERS OF THE *Washington Post* must have been uneasy about a December 1984 article headlined "Army Sprayed Germs on Unsuspecting Travelers." The article described a recently unclassified report about a secret army test twenty years earlier at Washington National Airport. Bacteria had been sprayed from specially constructed suitcases to assess whether an enemy could do the same with more lethal germs. (Conclusion: It could.)[1]

The report was one of the few that describe individual tests that have trickled out of the army's archives. In 1977, the army acknowledged having conducted 239 such tests, and each new disclosure has revealed previously unknown details. Although these tests took place years earlier, the disclosures are of contemporary interest. The army retains the right to perform vulnerability tests now and in the future. The reports show how they might be, or are being, conducted.

The periodic revelations have not been limited to testing with supposedly nontoxic simulants. In 1985, a British newspaper obtained documents about a joint British–United States–Canadian exercise in the 1950s off the coast of Scotland. A trawler unknowingly entered the test area into a fog of pneumonic plague bacilli. The crew was not notified. If "distress calls" had been sent from the trawler, according to the documents, the navy was instructed to have a nearby ship's doctor board the vessel and administer a vaccine. The documents indicate that since no distress calls were heard, the officials assumed that the aerosol plague droplets dispersed before causing harm. When asked by reporters in 1985 about the incident, British Ministry of Defense officials declined to comment because their information remained "so highly classified."[2]

Mounting concern about biological warfare, and defensive activities like vulnerability testing, are reflected in the increasing number of newspaper and magazine stories about the subject. Since the beginning of the Reagan administration, doubts have been expressed about the viability of the 1972 Biological Weapons Convention. In 1984 a crescendo of articles, reports, and proposed policy changes raised questions about the intentions of the United States and the Soviet Union to maintain existing restrictions on biological warfare preparations. In December alone a rush of news items intensified interest in biological warfare activities.

Three incidents during the closing weeks of 1984 underlined this concern. The *Washington Post* article on the spraying of the National Airport was one. It described how five aerosol generators in specially built suitcases were used to spray bacteria. According to the report, "test team members, each with a suitcase sampler, selected a passenger at random at the entrance to the North Terminal and covertly collected air samples in close proximity to the passenger during his stay at the Terminal." For some passengers, "the calculated exposures would have been massive doses if that many pathogenic organisms had been inhaled."[3]

The document confirms that if smallpox germs had been sprayed, passengers would have carried them around the country, and "numerous secondary cases of smallpox could be expected from extensive exposure of people to the primary cases before diagnosis was made." Evidently none of the passengers suspected anything unusual about the average-looking men who were following them around with suitcases, secretly spraying and measuring them for concentrations of bacteria. The report concludes that aerosols of biological agents like the smallpox virus "can be disseminated with covert-type devices."[4]

In response to inquiries about the newly released document, an army spokesman said that the test had been listed among others in a report for Congress in 1977, and that there were "no new developments to report."[5] The test had indeed been listed, although details were not previously known. The description of the test was like those in the reports of the other tests discussed in earlier chapters. The army's position about the test at Washington National Airport was the same as for the others—that no harm was caused, and the bacteria used were entirely innocuous.

Thus, once again given the opportunity to acknowledge what many health experts believe, that the simulants used in vulnerability testing program could cause harm, the army demurred. Nor would it renounce the possibility of their use again in open air tests in populated areas. The army's spokesman simply declined further comment, according to the news story.

Like the hundreds of other vulnerability tests conducted in populated areas, this one reconfirms the fact that a biological warfare attack can easily be launched. It appears to sustain the view of critics of the testing program that defense against an attack with biological agents is virtually impossible, and that vulnerability testing can add no useful information. Yet the army admits that it is now conducting open air tests to perform "threat evaluation" (whether in heavily populated areas remains speculative).[6]

Another incident relating to the biological warfare issue occurred in the context of a newspaper column the day before the airport-spraying story appeared. Columnist Jack Anderson had written that the Soviet Union was developing weapons in violation of the 1972 Convention.[7] This was not the first time such a claim appeared in the press. Anderson had referred to the subject in a previous column, as did the April and May *Wall Street Journal* series of articles that purported to show that the Soviets were using genetic engineering techniques to develop biological weaponry.

On close examination, the *Journal's* contentions appeared to be based on rumor and scanty evidence, as discussed in Chapter 10. But now, Anderson claimed that the Central Intelligence Agency had found new evidence to bolster earlier suspicions. In fact, nothing that Anderson described in December as "more information" differed essentially from the material eight months earlier in the *Journal*. The Central Intelligence Agency, he wrote, "has learned that the Soviets are investigating a number of specific compounds 'which appear to have considerable potential as BW agents.' " The information had come largely from "a key Soviet source who defected." Yet the suppositions in Anderson's column were all part of the more expansive series in the *Wall Street Journal*, which was far more alarmist than the evidence warranted. Anderson raised the pitch of the alarm by claiming that the Soviets have mastered "gene-splicing techniques as ominous as the atom-splitting discoveries that led to the nuclear bomb."

The third issue concerning biological warfare that received public attention in December concerned the new test facilities that the army planned to build at Dugway Proving Ground in Utah. As discussed in Chapter 11, among other expanded facilities the army intended to construct an "aerosol test lab" for research on hazardous viruses and bacteria. The purpose would be to handle "substantial volumes of toxic biological aerosol agents."[8] The project received national attention when Senator James Sasser expressed worry that it could be used "to test offensive biological and toxin weapons."[9] No less worrisome, as pointed out previously, is the way in which the army sought approval for its project.

After Senator Sasser brought the issue to the public's attention, several scientists made clear their doubts that such a sophisticated laboratory would be needed to conduct purely defensive biological research. The president-elect of the American Society for Microbiology and professor at Tufts University, Moselio Schaechter, noted that whatever the army's intention, the stakes would be raised. The capacity of the laboratory would allow for either defensive or offensive work, he said. "By and large, there is no way to tell the difference. They are exactly the same."[10]

In May 1985, the immediate fate of the project became uncertain when a federal judge ruled that the army could not proceed with construction because it had not produced a proper environmental impact statement. But no one doubted that the army would continue with its expansion plans for the overall biological warfare program.

Who Is Responsible?

When the public learned in the 1970s about the army's secret tests, the reaction was indignation and anger. "Incredible," "reckless," "unconscionable," said public officials and newspaper editorials.[11] Norman Cousins called for punishment of the people in charge: "It is necessary to bring to trial all those responsible for illness or deaths caused in the aerosol poisoning experiments or in any other scientific activities carried on outside the law. Criminality is criminality and murder is murder and must be deprived of their shelters."[12]

All this asumes that behind the program has been a cadre of dark characters engaging in criminal activity. I have not found this to be the case. The program was wrong from the start, never should have been carried on, and most emphatically should not be taking place now. But the driving force derives not from demented or malicious individuals, but from a reflexive mind-set grounded in fear of an enemy.

The fear has generated ill-conceived responses in the biological warfare area as elsewhere. A fixation with national security can warp essential values of the nation's political culture. Whether labeled "McCarthyism," "cold-war mentality" or, more recently, the "evil empire" syndrome, such a fixation cannot be in the nation's interest. Instead of protecting the public, it encourages an ethos that permits suspension of safety and ethical considerations by government officials.

As for would-be "culprits," they can be found all along the way. They start perhaps with scientists during World War II, like Fildes and Sarles, who misjudged the ability of anthrax to remain a threat for generations. These scientists have left a legacy of forbidden areas of continuing infectivity in Britain and the United States. Or perhaps "guilt" begins with the American biological warfare officials, like Hill and Victor, who after the war connived to protect their Japanese counterparts. In return for information about the germ warfare experiments in which thousands of prisoners were murdered, the Japanese perpetrators were never brought to trial.

In consideration of the earlier germ warfare testing over American cities, there are names aplenty. Phillips, Wolpert, and Creasy ran many of the tests, as they acknowledged in the Nevin trial. Documents indicate that they and other named officials knew about possible risks to the public as far back as the early 1950s. Carlton Brown, at a conference in 1960 attended by germ warfare experts, made light of a scientist's worries about the safety of testing with an army simulant. Whoever has been in charge of the chemical and biological warfare programs in any era has known about the tests. Army spokesmen have been cited throughout the book who have denied that the tests caused harm before, or would cause harm now.

This does not make any of these people criminals. Rather they may be described more aptly as cogs in a bureaucratic machine that operates according to a skewed belief system. These beliefs are typified by a scientist now at Fort Detrick who condones the tests and observes that in order to protect the country, "we have to do some things that are possibly not the nicest things."

Fear of Soviet germ warfare activities prompted the earlier tests, and a revived fear of Soviet activities has encouraged their resumption. One question of grave importance is whether these fears are warranted. Another is whether spraying people with germs is justifiable in any case. To the first question, based on available evidence, the answer is doubtful. To the second, no matter what the evidence, the answer is no.

A Dangerous Mind-Set

In recent years thousands of army veterans and civilians have made claims against the government relating to its testing programs. Most sought compensation for damages resulting from atomic tests in the 1950s and 1960s. Until 1984 none had won a court decision. In May of that year, however, for the first time, a federal judge found the government negligent in the way it had conducted above-ground atomic tests in Nevada, and ruled that radioactive fallout had caused nine people to die of cancer. They were among a group chosen in a test case to represent 1,192 alleged victims.[13]

Relatives of other people who died of leukemia claim that the victims had lived downwind from an underground atomic test site in Utah from which radiation leaked in 1962. A government study indicates a child leukemia rate in that area as ten times the national average.[14] The long-term consequences of the atomic tests should also serve as a lesson about open air testing with biological agents. No one knows how many people may have been harmed by the previous biological warfare tests, and no one knows how many might be harmed by tests now and in the future. Does the army want to take the chance again?

In view of the unpleasant image the army has created for itself on the Dugway issue and its problems with the atomic claimants, all the more should it wish to clarify its vulnerability testing policies. At the least, the army should reverse its position that humans in the target area of germ warfare tests are not considered experimental subjects. Call these people what you like, but they should not have to breathe in "nontoxic simulants" without their consent, no matter how harmless the army thinks its tests are.

Responsibility for greater clarity lies as well with the scientific experts who have been making policy recommendations. This applies to scientists at both ends of the policy spectrum. The scientists who wrote the 1984 report recommending that simulants be used in outdoor testing seem oblivious to the risks that such tests present to the exposed population. Those who oppose the use of highly toxic germs at the proposed Dugway facility are equally careless. By urging that simulants be used there instead of pathogens, they permit an inference that simulants are harmless and may safely be used in more populated areas. Experts in both camps should defer to the wisdom that simulant testing is risky. This should be among the principal considerations of any proposal concerning further testing.

At present, the way the Defense Department interprets federal legislation dealing with human subjects can only raise concerns. A mind-set for open air tests, but with little concern about their effects on the exposed population—as appears in the several recent government reports cited in chapter 11—is also worrisome. Finally, the army's apparent lack of respect for congressional oversight of its expanding biological warfare research, as expressed by Senators Sasser and Hatfield, prompts even more skepticism.

Upon learning of the recommendations for outdoor testing and about the Dugway episode, former Congressman Andrew Maguire urged a "full congressional investigation," saying that "there appears to be activity underway or planned which has not been fully explained by the army and is not clearly understood by the Congress." Maguire, who served on the Health and Environment Subcommittee of the House Energy and Commerce Committee, is now vice-president of the World Resources Institute. Addressing the question of open air testing with biological agents, Maguire condemned "loopholes in current law which could be exploited by those who wish to test."[15]

If the public is as little protected from biological weapons testing as seems to be the case, corrective legislation should be enacted. Protection should not depend exclusively on the good will of the army or the scientific community. Whether through legislation intended to protect the environment, human subjects, or both, explicit safeguards are called for.

A few years ago Jeremy Rifkin testified before Congress and the National Institutes of Health, anticipating the army's use of genetic engineering in its biological warfare program. "They said it would never be used for this," he recalls, but now it is. "They're going to want to do open air testing too; I have no doubt about it." Some people view Rifkin as intrusive. But he can hardly be faulted for having said "we need some discussion this time before it happens."[16]

Saul Hormats, who had been director of development for the Army Chemical Corps until 1971, is troubled by recent U.S. policies. He was familiar with the earlier germ warfare tests while they were being conducted, and at the time did not feel uncomfortable about them. "Our whole attitude in matters of this kind was different then," Hormats says, "but today I would say this sort of thing would be reprehensible." He emphasizes, however, that "I'm speaking of me today. You have a lot of people in the Pentagon who just don't give a damn, and that bothers me." Although Hormats is no longer in government service, he follows events closely in the chemical and biological warfare areas. He is convinced that there are people in the Pentagon who "are planning for some damn reason to reinstitute BW, and are quite likely to reinstitute" testing over heavily populated areas. "I think these are irresponsible actions," he says, "and I can't understand why the Pentagon is up to this sort of thing."[17]

A policy option that allows germs to be sprayed on unsuspecting citizens is a remnant of a discredited ethos. It is no more justifiable than a policy that would allow exposure of people to "harmless" levels of radiation after nuclear detonations, in order to simulate realistic conditions. The issue of vulnerability testing raises a fundamental question about the values of this society—whether the citizenry should ever be appropriately considered as experimental guinea pigs.

To the extent that testing with simulant bacteria and chemicals involves inhalation, ingestion, or other contact by humans, calling such activity harmless or innocuous is illusory. One of the lessons of the past tests should have been the demonstrated uncertainty of the effects of supposedly harmless agents on the exposed population.

The army continues to claim that the agents it used in past tests *were* and *are* harmless. It therefore uses the same ones in current tests. Even if different simulants are used, on what basis can anyone be sure they are harmless? In any case, what moral right permits the government to treat citizens as unwitting subjects?

In considering the nation's expanding defensive biological warfare research, including the outdoor testing program, a Pentagon official said: "There's no need to restrain us from doing the best job we can." Another was more succinct: "Trust us."[18] As we have learned from experience, such assurances are not enough.

Notes

1. Ken Ringle, "Army Sprayed Germs on Unsuspecting Travelers," *Washington Post,* December 5, 1984, p. B-1.

2. David Leigh and Paul Lashmar, "British Germ Bomb Sprayed Trawler," *The Observer* (London), July 21, 1985, p. 1.

3. "Miscellaneous Publication 7," Study US65SP (U), United States Army Biological Laboratories, Fort Detrick, July 1965, pp. 57, 62. A copy of the report was provided by the Church of Scientology, which had obtained it through a Freedom of Information Act request.

4. Ibid., and Ringle, "Army Sprayed Germs," p. B-8.

5. Ringle, "Army Sprayed Germs," p. B-8.

6. U.S. Department of Defense. "Biological Defense Program," Report to the Committee on Appropriations, House of Representatives, Washington, D.C., May 1986, chap. 1, p. 10 (mimeographed).

7. Jack Anderson, "Soviets Push Biological-Weapons Work," *Washington Post,* December 4, 1984, p. B-15.

8. Wayne Biddle, "Fund for Army Biological Warfare Unit Approved," *New York Times,* December 7, 1984, p. A-23.

9. Letter from Senator James Sasser to Secretary of Defense Caspar W. Weinberger, October 31, 1984.

10. R. Jeffrey Smith, "New Army Biowarfare Lab Raises Concerns, *Science* 226, no. 4679 (December 7, 1984): p. 1178.

11. See editorials and news items in the *San Francisco Chronicle,* December 24 and 26, 1976, and September 18, 1979.

12. Norman Cousins, "How the U.S. Used Its Citizens as Guinea Pigs," *Saturday Review,* November 10, 1979, p. 10.

13. Ivor Peterson, "U.S. Ruled Negligent in A-Tests Followed by Nine Cancer Deaths," *New York Times,* May 11, 1984, p. A-1.

14. *New York Times,* May 16, 1984, p. A-7.

15. Interview, May 15, 1985.

16. Interview, March 25, 1985.

17. Interview, September 13, 1985.

18. Cited in John Hubner, "The Hidden Arms Race," *West* (Sunday Magazine of the *San Jose Mercury News*), April 15, 1984, p. 37.

APPENDICES

Appendix 1

The following passages are from a document furnished by the Office, Chief of Legislative Liaison, Department of the Army, Office of the Secretary of the Army, Washington, D.C., March 8, 1977.

Information for Members of Congress: U.S. Army in the U.S. Biological Warfare (BW) Program

Testing

The policy of the United States regarding biological warfare between 1941 and 1969 was to first deter its use against the United States and its Allies, and secondly to retaliate if deterrence failed. The US BW policy required the development of a retaliatory capability utilizing pathogenic agents. Fundamental to the development of a deterrent strategy was the need for a thorough study and analysis of our vulnerability to both an overt and covert attack while concomitantly examining the full range of retaliatory options. This required extensive research and development to determine precisely our vulnerability, the efficacy of our protective measures, and the tactical and strategic capability of various delivery systems and agents.

The testing program consisted of two phases. Phase one involved the use of simulants; phase two involved the use of pathogens and included volunteers.

Both biological and non-biological simulants were used. The biological simulants were *Serratia Marcescens, Aspergillus Fumigatus,* and *Bacillus Globigii.* Non-biological simulants included such items as fluorescent particles, sulphur dioxide, and soap bubbles. In the biological and non-biological simulant tests, public safety was a major item of consideration. Agents and material were selected that were considered by the scientific community to be totally safe.

To date, research has shown that a total of 160 tests [sic]* utilizing simulants were conducted at 66 locations within the continental United

*Another report by the army listed 239 field tests with "anti-personnel biological simulants involving public domain." See Department of the Army, "U.S. Army Activity in the U.S. Biological Warfare Programs," Vol. 2, February 24, 1977 mimeograph.

The documents reproduced in these Appendices contain spelling and syntactical errors that appear in the original copies.

States, Alaska and Hawaii. The specific dates, locations, and substances used are contained in a comprehensive report which is available on request.

The simulant, *Serratia Marcescens* (SM), has been discussed extensively in the media as contributing to an increased incidence of pneumonia in Calhoun County, Alabama, and to the death of an individual following the vulnerability test conducted at San Francisco in September 1950. At the time the tests were conducted, SM was believed by the medical community to be harmless and totally suitable for use in the ongoing vulnerability test program. The first suspected relationship between SM and increased incidents of disease was reported in an article "Infection Due to Chromobacteria," published in the Archives of Internal Medicine (VOL. 88, 1951).

In 1951, Dr. Richard P. Wheat, M.D., et al., reported on eleven cases seen in a San Francisco hospital from September 1950 to February 1951. The following is extracted from the "Comment" section of the referenced article:

> "Instrumentation of the urinary tract had been performed in every case, and the Chromobacterium probably was introduced by these procedures. An epidemiological study failed to reveal the route of infection in detail.
>
> That so many cases of urinary-tract infection by this unusual organism should have been observed was not surprising, since the obstructed and instrumented urinary passages are fertile soil for the multiplication of bacteria that are not commonly the cause of disease elsewhere. A contributing factor was the use of multiple antibiotics, which eliminated all the usual organisms that are responsible for infection of these organs and permitted the ready implantation of the highly antibiotic- and sulfonamide-resistant Chromobacterium.
>
> Similar invasion of various organs by bacteria resistant to one or more antibiotics, and not usually the cause of disease in the involved system, has become commonplace in patients treated with these agents. Such invasion has been most frequently observed in cases of superinfection of the urinary tract by members of the Pseudomonas and Proteus group. It is evident that the ever-widening use of antimicrobial agents will be associated with the discovery of infectious disease caused by a wide variety of unusual micro-organisms."

Therefore, it is concluded that the association of SM infections with the San Francisco test appeared coincidental since, (1) no other hospitals reported similar infections, and (2) all the other patients reported in the Wheat article had urinary tract infections, a well recognized complication of urinary catherization.

Because of apparent concern over a possible link between its San Francisco test in 1950 and the incidence of *Serratia Marcescens* infections in the Stanford Hospital in 1952, the Army requested a group of eminent scientists to review the available information and provide recommendations on the future use of SM. The four civilian consultants from Communicable Disease Center, USPHS; Department of Health, City of New York; Graduate School, Ohio State University; and Microbiological Institute, National Institutes of Health, USPHS analysis and recommendations were:

1. Experimental work in BW outside of the laboratory is impossible

without the use of simulants. Simulants must be organisms having biological characteristics, other than pathogenicity, as nearly identical as possible to BW agents under study. An ideal simulant has not yet been found. Avirulent strains of recognized pathogenic organisms should not be used in routine field trials if the necessary information can be obtained in any other possible way. Ideally a simulant should be an organism that has never been associated with a human disease and is not capable of growth in the human body. It must also be readily recognizable and recoverable by simple means.

2. Since the early days of bacteriology, SM has been the most commonly used organism for studying the dissemination of bacteria in air. Until recent years, there have been no reports of human illness associated with this organism in spite of its extensive use. In 1946 at Fort Detrick, four cases of minor illness of short duration were discovered in association with heavy exposures to SM. Reference is made to "Illness in Man Following Inhalation of Serratia Marcescens;" Paine, Tom F.; Journal of Infectious Diseases; Nov–Dec 1946; Vol 79. A current survey among Fort Detrick personnel reveals only two cases of similarly insignificant illness among all those exposed while working with the organism.

3. The data in the referenced article describing the experience in San Francisco are incomplete as to the primary relation of the SM isolated from the patients and their illnesses, except in the case of one patient who died with bacterial endocarditis and SM bacteremia. With this single exception, the finding of SM in these cases was not shown to have influenced the clinical course of the patients' illnesses.

4. On the basis of our study, we conclude that SM is so rarely a cause of illness and the illness resulting is predominantly so trivial, that its use as a simulant should be continued, even over populated areas, when such studies are necessary to the advancement of the BW program.

5. The program at Fort Detrick in the search for better simulants should be actively pursued. If a more desirable simulant is discovered, it should then replace SM.

6. In future tests over populated areas, it would be desirable to institute prior and subsequent studies in a few hospitals to determine whether the report previously referred to was purely coincidental or whether the recovery of SM from patients was related to BW field tests.

All available evidence continues to indicate that SM is an opportunistic organism which infects those individuals who are debilitated or have a reduced immune response. However, even in light of the findings of the review committee and to avoid exposing such population to SM, the Fort Detrick Safety Director established a policy whereby the use of SM was not authorized if the simulant was likely to enter a hospital or a sanitarium.

Likewise, the health data for Monroe County (Key West) and Bay County (Panama City) do not support the Newsday allegations of pneumonia cases according to Dr. C. Prather, Florida's Health Officer, as given to the National Observer Weekend Edition (26 December 1976). A state-wide influenza epidemic hit Florida in 1952 and 1953 with a corresponding increase in pneumonia. According to Dr. Prather, the incidence of pneumonia in Bay County (Panama City) was relatively constant in 1951, 1952, and 1953. The Director of the Center for Disease Control also states that there was no evidence to associate the use of SM with any reported increase in pneumonia deaths.

Additionally, SM has been used medically as a bacterial tracer from 1937 to 1969 with the results having been published in highly reputable medical journals as late as February 1969. The following are examples:

1. SM painted on gums to determine the source of bacteremia following dental extraction. No ill effects were seen in spite of documented bacteremia in 18 patients.

2. SM implanted to demonstrate bladder colonization from the urethral meatus after catherization.

3. SM implanted in the oropharynx to demonstrate the bacterial clearing effect of the tracheobronchial tree.

The use of *Bacillus globigii* (BG) has likewise received extensive review from the medical community concerning the safety of the simulant for use in open air tests. In all cases, it has been the consensus that it is suitable for use in open air tests. The most recent comments available came from Surgeon General of the USPHS in 1970 and the Director of the Center for Disease Control. The Center for Disease Control also has no data suggesting that BG is causing human disease. In his letter the Surgeon General stated: "Careful studies have been performed to determine the pathogenicity of this organism. There is no evidence of infection in man or experimental animals following exposure to spores, even in massive doses. . . ."

Conclusion

The Army activities in the BW program were conducted under the safest and most controlled conditions possible and in accordance with national policy directives and guidance.

Appendix 2

The following passages are from a report by the Department of the Army, "U.S. Army Activity in the U.S. Biological Warfare Programs," Vol. 2, February 24, 1977 (mimeographed), pp. 109–10. As in the document cited in Appendix 1, the safety of the biological warfare simulants is stressed. See U.S. Congress: Senate Hearings before the Subcommittee on Health and Scientific Research of the Committee on Human Resources, *Biological Testing Involving Human Subjects by the Department of Defense, 1977*, March 8 and May 23, 1977 (Washington, D. C.: Government Printing Office, 1977).

Simulant Testing. Every effort expended in open-air testing was first directed towards the utilization of simulants to obtain the necessary data for evaluation. Biological simulants are defined as living microorganisms, not normally capable of causing infection, representing the physical and biological characteristics of potential microbiological agents and considered medically safe to operating personnel and surrounding communities. In addition, certain selected inorganic materials such as flourescent particles, were also utilized to obtain aerosol dissemination data.

The two most commonly used biological simulants were *Serratia marcescens* (SM) and *Bacillus subtillis variant niger*, normally referred to as *Bacillus globigii* (BG). The most commonly used flourescent particle was an inorganic complex, zinc cadmium sulfide (Zn CdS).

Bacillus globigii (BG). BG is considered ubiquitous in nature. It can be readily cultured from hay, dust, milk and water. It was and is still considered by medical authorities to be harmless (nonpathogenic) to man. The utilization of BG in aerosol testing in open-air tests were reaffirmed as recently as 1970 by The Surgeon General of the US Public Health Service who indicated as a result of his directed literature search and consultation with health experts, that there is no evidence of infection in man or experimental animals following exposure to BG spores, even in massive doses.

Serratia marcescens (SM) is a motile, nonsporulating, gramnegative bacillus which may produce a red pigment especially when grown at room temperature. It is commonly found in water, food and sewage and sometimes can be isolated from feces and sputum of apparently healthy people. It was used as a bacterial marker with little risk up to 1969 because of its avirulant nature. In 1969, it was recognized as having limited pathogenic capability and should not be used for study of experimental infections in man because of the

167

assumed role as an opportunist, producing disease if man is exposed to large doses and/or when the body defenses are weakened by age, debilitatory disease, drug abuse or antibiotics. A summary report on SM is at Appendix II.

Aspergillus fumigatus (AF) was a fungus simulant used on four occasions from 1950–1953 and abandoned when antifungal agents were removed from the BW program. It is ubiquitous in nature and can be cultured from soil, water, air, food stuffs, animals waste products and most human body orifices. AF is considered an opportunist causing aspergillosis in debilitated persons.

Rationale for Vulnerability Testing. In the beginning and continuing throughout the BW Program, there was a paucity of scientific and engineering knowledge and principles related to the vulnerability of the US and/or its personnel to BW attacks both covert and overt. Vulnerability testing was required to provide information on the agents likely to be used, means of disseminating agents, sizes of areas that could be attacked, environmental effects on agents, obstructive effects of buildings and terrain on agents, ability to detect and identify agents areas of the US and for its forces most likely to be attacked, the extent of damage possible, and data to devise physical and mathematical models to be used as substitutes for live, open air testing.

Appendix 3

Among the scientists who refuted the army's contention that its simulant testing program was safe, two submitted written reports to the Senate Subcommittee on Health and Scientific Research in connection with the 1977 Hearings. Excerpts from the reports, by Dr. Stephen Weitzman of the State University of New York at Stony Brook and by Dr. J. Mehsen Joseph of the Maryland State Department of Health and Mental Hygiene, are reproduced in the following pages.

Testimony to be Delivered to the Senate Subcommittee on Health and Scientific Research of the Human Resources Committee on May 23, 1977, by Stephen Weitzman, M.D., Assistant Professor of Microbiology, State University of New York at Stony Brook.

I am pleased to be given the opportunity to testify today on a very important subject involving biological warfare research in this country. I have carefully studied the two-volume, unclassified Army report dated February 24, 1977 entitled, "U.S. Army Activity in the U.S. Biological Warfare Programs". I will use this as my main source to comment on the history, nature and extent of production and testing of biological simulants and pathogens.

Before starting, I would like to present my credentials in this field. I received my M.D. degree from New York University Medical School in 1969. After three years of clinical training at Montefiore Hospital and Medical Center in the Bronx, New York, I became a Diplomate of the American Board of Internal Medicine. Following two additional years of clinical and laboratory experience, I was certified by the American Board of Medicine in the subspecialty of Infectious Disease. In 1975 I was appointed to the Department of Microbiology as an Assistant Professor. I am the principal investigator on a grant from the National Science Foundation to study problems in immunology, the course director for the Microbiology course at the Stony Brook Medical School, and Infectious Disease Consultant at the Northport V.A. Hospital in Long Island. In addition, I have published a number of articles in both the scientific and infectious disease journals.

Reviewing the Army report leads to a consideration of two points. The first raises questions about the morality and safety of several large-scale tests that the Army conducted on civilian populations without informed consent. The second point involves an examination of the military and political limitations and problems inherent in pursuing biological warfare research. Finally, I would like to make several proposals which hopefully would prevent any past difficulties from recurring.

The most disturbing aspects of the Army's biological warfare program, 1950–1969, concerns the open-air tests conducted on a number of U.S. cities between 1950 and 1966. In particular, the San Francisco test has received a lot of attention in the press since it first appeared in the Long Island newspaper, *NEWSDAY* on November 21, 1976. In addition, the Army report spends 11 pages defending this test (II-E-1 to II-E-5, and F-1 to I-F-2). (Note: all numbers in parenthesis refer to pages in the 2/24/77 Army report). Since the San Francisco open-air test seems to be the center of some controversy, I would like to discuss it in some detail and use it as a model for examining a number of problems inherent in doing biological warfare research.

In brief, the test conducted in 1950 involved exposing the city of San Francisco to an aerosolized live bacteria called *Serratia marcescens*. The Army's rationale for carrying out this large-scale, open air test was to increase our knowledge "related to the vulnerability of the U.S. and/or its personnel to biological warfare attacks both covert and overt" (E-7). The live bacteria *Serratia marcescens* was considered a biological simulant "defined as living micro-organisms, not normally capable of causing infection . . ." (E-6). There are three main objections to be raised at this point:

1) Our understanding of a biological simulant, that is, a live bacteria that does not produce disease, is based on our past experiences with that agent under *certain definite conditions*. If these conditions change, the bacteria can cause disease. There are at least two components to these conditions: One is the number of bacteria and the second is the state of health of the people exposed. Early studies revealed that exposure of a healthy person to a low number of *Serratia marcescens* (1000–10,000 bacteria) never led to infections. What was not known was whether exposure to large numbers of *Serratia marcescens* (10–100 million bacteria) could cause infection; nor what the response of a sick person would be to *Serratia*. Since these tests were carried out it has been learned that an increase in the number of *Serratia marcescens* can cause disease in a healthy person and that *Serratia marcescens* can cause serious disease in sick people (see pages F-3, II-E-3, F-4). In fact, most major hospitals today have recurring problems with *Serratia marcescens* infections in hospitalized sick patients. While it is true that in 1950 the scientific and medical professions were unaware of these facts, the main point to learn is that experience gained in controlled, experimental laboratory situations cannot be assumed to be applicable to large-scale tests on big cities. Aerosolization might lead to dispersion of organisms but the possibility cannot be ruled out that peculiar wind conditions or ventilation systems in buildings might concentrate organisms, exposing people to high doses of bacteria. In any event, these factors are beyond control. In addition, unlike the individual volunteers used in laboratory experiments, the population of a city is quite heterogeneous. Infants, elderly person, people with cancer, people with chronic lung disease, etc., are all found on the streets in a large city and their ability to fight off infection by *Serratia marcescens* is difficult to estimate. In summary, too many uncontrolled variables are present to consider vulnerability testing safe, of large civilian populations with a biological simulant.

2) A major objection which has to be made of the open-air experiments,

such as the one in San Francisco or in the New York City subways, is that they were carried out on people without informed consent. This action stands in dramatic contrast to other examples in which the Army used admirable and exemplary procedures in dealing with volunteers in Operation Whitecoat (Annex K). In addition, the Army took exceptional care in instituting safety procedures for personnel working on projects, for insuring against accidents during transportation, and for decontamination of facilities during demilitarization. A real contradiction can be seen here between the Army's concern for individual human life and the ethical problems of human experimentation in many situations, and yet the disregard for many of these same values in the vulnerability tests.

3) A question that is never really dealt with in any convincing detail in the Army report is the necessity for using actual cities for the open-air tests. It is unclear to me what additional information is gained by releasing bacteria in the New York City subways that cannot be gathered for example, by a similar experiment done in tunnels in a deserted mine. Similarly, aerosolization patterns could just as well have been analyzed using an unpopulated area. If reasons existed to do the testing in actual cities, nowhere are these reasons explained. The only unique information that can be concluded from these tests is that these cities are in fact vulnerable to biological warfare attack. This vulnerability is so obvious that it leads to a consideration of the major point I would like to make.

Since the offensive biological warfare research program was dismantled in 1969, there would seem to be little purpose in spending time analysing actions taken over 20 years ago. Still, some degree of biological warfare research continues in the Department of Defense with a budget in 1975–76 of close to $18,000,000 (Congressional Record-Senate; April 6, 1977, S5701). While this research emphasizes "defensive research", the distinction between "offensive" and "defensive" is often no more than a semantic one. This was realized as early as 1946: "It should be emphasized that while the main objective in all these endeavors was to develop methods for defending ourselves against possible enemy use of biological warfare agents, it was necessary to investigate offensive possibilities in order to learn what measures could be used for defense. . . . Accordingly, the problems of offense and defense were closely interlinked in all the investigations conducted" (A-5). That biological warfare research continues in this and probably other countries is disturbing. This problem was noted also in 1946: "It is important to note that, unlike the development of the atomic bomb and other secret weapons during the war, the development of agents for biological warfare is possible in many countries, large and small, without vast expenditures of money or the construction of huge production facilities. It is clear that the development of biological warfare could very well proceed in many countries, perhaps under the guise of legitimate medical or bacteriological research." . . .

In summary, I have tried to establish the following points:

1) Testing in offensive or defensive biological warfare research, and, in particularly large-scale, open-air testing, is unpredictable and thus potentially dangerous. Unique conditions develop which are distinct from the usual laboratory or hospital experience.

2) The Army acted irresponsibly in carrying out the vulnerability open-

air tests on large urban populations in the 1950's and 1960's. They ignored the ethical problem of informed consent and the potential health problem discussed in objection #1 on page 2 of this testimony.

3) The continuation of biological warfare research is not in the military interest of the United States since once the techniques are developed, biological warfare can be used by small countries, terrorist groups and individuals. The proliferation of biological warfare weaponry and techniques can only erode military advantages that the United States now has since biological agents are cheap to produce and can be delivered by a small force in a clandestine manner.

Based on these three points, I would make the following proposals:

1) If further biological warfare research is to be considered necessary because of the development of biological warfare techniques by foreign powers, then the work should be more strictly regulated by groups outside the Department of Defense than has been done in the past. These might include the Department of Health, Education and Welfare, Congressional Committees, and/or independent scientists. At a time when Federal guidelines are being established for regulating recombinant DNA research conducted in universities and industries, the same principle of providing outside checks and balances for Department of Defense biological warfare research would seem to be appropriate.

2) Finally, and most importantly, the United States should intensify efforts to ban biological warfare research internationally and consider integrating such a policy into its strategic arms limitation treaty negotiations.

Statement on the Use of the Simulant Serratia Marcescens in Aerosol Studies of Human Population Centers

My name is J. Mehsen Joseph, Ph.D., and I am Director of the Laboratories Administration, Maryland State Department of Health and Mental Hygiene, and Assistant Professor of Microbiology, University of Maryland, Baltimore, Maryland. . . .

Since 1913 when the first case of Serratia infection in man was described, isolated reports have stressed the potential pathogenicity of this organism for man. In 1962 the Communicable Disease Center pointed out the nosocomial nature of most Serratia marcescens infections. Several hospital outbreaks involving urinary tract infections and respiratory tract infections and two epidemics in nurseries for newborn infants have been described. Infections also have been noted to occur at the site of indwelling urinary and intravenous catheters and after lumbar punctures or peritoneal dialysis. Previous antibiotic therapy and underlying chronic debilitating disease may also predispose to serious Serratia infection. Urinary tract infection has been the most frequent site of Serratia infections but the epidemiology of such hospital outbreaks is still unclear and any attempts to determine the source of the organism has been unrevealing. However, most patients had indwelling catheterization and urinary tract abnormality. Also, Serratia marcescens is isolated frequently from the respiratory tract but these isolations are infrequently of clinical significance. Hospital outbreaks of respiratory infection are usually associated with Serratia contamination of respiratory equipment. Associated clinical illness was either pneumonia, empyema, or lung abscess.

Prior to 1960 Serratia marcescens was considered a common garden variety microorganism which was so benign that it was not capable of producing clinical illness in man in its own right. Because of its apparent nonpathogenic potential and its characteristic red pigmentation and ease of isolation, Serratia marcescens was commonly used as a tracer bacterium in numerous studies. It was intentionally spread in hospitals to study bacterial drifting and settling as an aid to understanding the spread of hospital cross-infections. Classical experiments in epidemiology were routinely conducted to demonstrate to students the basic principle of establishing the index case of infection by a microorganism. Aerosolization of the test organism was used in courses in Microbiology to demonstrate bacteriological air sampling techniques. The organism was intentionally painted on the gums of patients to demonstrate its passage from the oral cavity to the blood stream following dental manipulation and/or extraction. This organism has been used also by high school students in science fair projects without regard to its potential pathogenicity.

Of particular significance is the occurrence in 1958 of a condition referred to as "Red Diaper Syndrome" in a child born at the University of Wisconsin Hospital. The child was cultured and found to have an overwhelming growth of the red pigmented Serratia marcescens in the intestinal tract. Exhaustive studies of the child's family failed to reveal carriers of the organism. Epidemiological sleuthing uncovered the fact that the organism was being used at that time in a study of aerosol techniques in a biochemistry laboratory within the hospital and in an adjoining building where genetic studies were being conducted. Aerosol spread from these sources could have accounted for the colonization of the intestinal tract of the infant soon after birth. Apparently the organism established itself in the child's intestine and replaced the normal flora, but the child continued in excellent health and required almost one year of treatment to eliminate this bacterium.

An experiment conducted in 1960 in a London hospital also aroused a great deal of concern over the use of S. marcescens as a tracer microorganism. In attempting to prove an hypothesis that Staphylococcus aureus (a bacterium associated with hospital-acquired infection) was spread from floor-to-floor up the elevator shaft by movement of elevator, the tracer organism Serratia marcescens was aerosolized near the elevator door on the lower floor of the hospital and air sampling was done on the upper floors. In time, S. marcescens was detected in the area around the elevator shaft on each floor. What was not expected was the occurrence of several cases of S. marcescens necrotizing pneumonia among hospitalized patients presumably by aerosol transmission. Soon thereafter the use of S. marcescens as an indicator organism ceased in many countries, including the United States.

Even though Serratia marcescens is often regarded as a nonpathogen, or of low virulence for healthy individuals, it is found occasionally in conditions where host resistance is diminished (postoperative patients, burn cases, diabetics, cancer patients, steroid therapy), or in conditions predisposing to bacterial infection (frequent catheterization, malformation or obstruction of the urinary tract). Prolonged antibiotic therapy seems to favor the emergence of highly antibiotic resistant strains of S. marcescens. Generally the bacterium is considered an "opportunist". It is difficult to assess how much bacterial invasion has contributed to the underlying disease in many cases. Its presence in clinical materials is more frequent than generally suspected because of our failure to properly identify the bacterium due to the false belief that it is an obligate pigment former. Pigmentation is demonstrable in only about 20–30 per cent of the strains isolated from patients.

It should be reemphasized that infections with S. marcescens occur mainly in hospitalized individuals with some underlying disease. The mode of transmission has not been sufficiently elucidated but contaminated hands and instruments, as well as droplet aerosols, have been incriminated. It probably spreads like other hospital-acquired bacteria. Infection may or may not cause clinical disease, and a fatal outcome is very rare.

At the time the simulated testing was done in San Francisco by the Army, Serratia marcescens was considered an innocuous saprophytic water organism which was nonpathogenic to man or animals, but was occasionally recovered from comprimised hospitalized patients. Since 1960, however, infections due to this organism have been reported with increasing frequency in association with urinary tract infections, pneumonia, empyema, lung abscess, wound infection, meningitis, septicemia and endocarditis. The ability of S. marcescens to cause infection was once thought to be limited to patients with chronic debilitating disorders, but it is now clear that there are many predisposing factors such as broad spectrum antibiotic therapy, diabetes, indwelling catheters, mechanical ventilation therapy and corticosteroid therapy. This knowledge reemphasizes the hazard in using S. marcescens as a tracer organism in experimental studies of aerosols and related experiments involving humans.

No longer can we consider the disease potential of an organism simply a property in its own right, nor as an interaction of a parasite with a healthy host, but as a consequence of interaction with a compromised individual. Secondary invasion must also be viewed with the same concern as regards primary infections because the consequences are equally hazardous and the former often result in prolonged hospitalization. Since it was known that a clear danger of S. marcescens infection existed for hospitalized and debilitated individuals, it is inconceivable and unconscionable that the organism would have been spread as an aerosol over unsuspecting masses of people, some of whom would have been at high risk. Whether or not the illnesses in which S. marcescens was isolated from hospitalized patients in the San Francisco area immediately following the testing in the early 1950's is impossible to establish with certainty because of the natural occurrence of this agent in the hospital environment and its wide distribution in nature.

Simulated environmental conditions, as well as simulated microorganisms, could have been employed and would have provided adequate information as to the airborne spread, drift, survival and consequent infection. Mass environmental exposure on the scale conducted by the Army was apparently unnecessary on its scientific merit and constituted an unjustifiable health hazard for a particular segment of the population. To rationalize the validity for the study would be sheer folly.

Respectfully submitted,
J. Mehsen Joseph, Ph.D.
May 20, 1977

Appendix 4

The following excerpts are from "Biological Defense Program," a report by the Department of Defense to the Committee on Appropriations of the House of Representatives, issued May 1986. The report discusses alleged Soviet biological warfare advances, the impact of biotechnology on biological warfare, and the inadequacy of U.S. defenses. Its principal effort is to justify a planned aerosol test facility in which powerful pathogens that could be used as biological weapons would be sprayed in a contained area.

In reviewing past and present biological warfare research, the report refers to field testing now taking place with the same simulants (*Bacillus subtilis* and *Serratia marcescens*) that had been used in the earlier outdoor tests. This is the first public admission that outdoor testing is now taking place with these bacteria.

Deficiencies in the Biological Defense Program

Defending against traditional biological warfare agents is understood more clearly than defending against the new generation of novel or biochemical agents. Even so, the United States cannot defend itself adequately against conventional biological warfare agents. This situation is due in part to terminating the biological program for all practical purposes in 1969. This lack of interest was based on the belief that biological warfare did not have great tactical application and the expectation that all States Parties would abide by the Convention. In the words of the 1970 White House press release when toxins were added to the 1969 renunciation of biological warfare: "The United States hopes that other nations will follow our example with respect to both biological and toxin weapons." The evidence of Soviet violations confirms that the opposite has resulted.

This causes particular concern over the current lack of capability to perform biological defensive testing and threat evaluation. The declining capability is exacerbated by the impacts of biotechnology. These concerns are causing an overall review of biological defense requirements. One of the deficiencies identified early is the lack of suitable laboratory space to conduct pathogenic agent testing of defense material and to evaluate the biological threat. Without comprehensive knowledge of the technical characteristics and operational application of potential threats there cannot be any solid foundation for defense. We will have only outmoded technology and speculation on which to base these crucial defenses for our fighting forces.

175

The Reason for Testing

A principal mission of Dugway Proving Ground is to perform operational and development testing for chemical warfare and biological defense equipment. The ultimate reason for having protective equipment is to protect our military personnel; the reason for testing is to determine whether the equipment works properly. If the testing is not conducted, or if it is conducted with simulants which do not adequately mimic threat agents, there is no assurance the protective equipment will function properly—when lives are at stake.

As a matter of sound operational practice, scientists and technicians concerned with biological defense testing use simulants whenever possible. Simulants have been used at the U.S. Army Dugway Proving Ground since 1943. Some experiments would not have been possible without simulants (for example, operational testing of defense systems by soldiers in the field). This extensive use of simulants in testing has provided critical information on the doctrine and use of biological defense material. However, lack of actual agent data to correlate with the simulant testing has left areas of uncertainty about the efficacy of mission-essential biological defense equipment and systems.

Use of Simulants for Testing

Biological defense equipment and systems can be divided into three operational categories: detection and identification, protection, and decontamination. The basic requirements associated with simulant testing (selection of simulant, validation of simulant for the specific test situation, and interpretation of test results) must be considered for each catetory. In some instances, a simulant suitable for testing one operational category will not be suitable for testing another. Each operational category must be tested against the various types of biological agents.

There is only one validated item available. *Bacillus subtilis var. niger* is an excellent simulant for anthrax *(Bacillus anthracis)*. Unfortunately, *Bacillus subtilis var. niger* partially fills only one (spore forming bacteria) of the four classes of conventional airborne biological agents. A limited amount of development and testing have been done with simulant vegetative bacteria (i.e., *Escherichia coli* and *Serratia marcescens*).

The best opportunity to replace toxic airborne biological materials with simulants is when testing protective equipment. Since the most common protective mechanism is a physical barrier the primary features to simulate are such things as particle size distribution, dispersal, agglomeration, and adhesion properties. *Bacillus subtilis var. niger* is useful for this within the limits mentioned above.

The next best opportunity is in testing decontamination equipment and procedures. This requires a simulant which is biologically active. Decontamination involves much more than simply washing or spraying a solution over the equipment. Unfortunately, it is not a "one size fits all" situation. Experience with decontaminating actual chemical and biological agents shows that the process is sensitive to many variables. Examples are the physical properties of the surface; the method of applying the decontaminant; the inherent nature of the agent; the medium or carrier materials for the agent; and the exposure or weathering time before, during, and after the decontamination process. For instance, physical removal is very dependent on the scrubbing equipment and techniques used. Since the impact of leaving a dirty spot can be severe, e.g., soldiers die, we must be sure the decontamination process selected is effective. But, since decontamination is extremely expensive in manpower, equipment and supplies, and especially time, we must also ensure the process selected is efficient and quick. The most commonly used simulant (*Bacillus subtilis var. niger,* above) is very resistant to decontamination, so test results are overly conservative. These test results lead to operational doctrine which requires troops to spend more effort during the decontamination process and remain in protective posture longer than necessary. We cannot afford to do this. The protective posture itself degrades fighting capability and this effect gets worse with time. The excessive loss of time and capability places US forces at an extreme disadvantage, especially in the rapid and extremely lethal battles we now face. These effects have recently been evaluated in a series of field trials. The overall result is losing 30–50% of the fighting capability.

The final operational category is detection. The student of current battle doctrine soon understands the overwhelming importance of knowing when chemical and biological agents arrive and where they are. It is often even more important to know they have not arrived and where the clean areas are. When we don't know, the only alternative to reckless exposure of soldiers is an overly conservative protective approach—suit up at any indication of trouble and stay that way till you are sure it's clear. Excessive protection creates a self-defeating situation as noted above in the decontamination discussion. Thus detecting biological agents is a very urgent and high payoff requirement, but testing biological agent detectors is difficult or impossible with existing simulants. The simulant must duplicate the specific biological, chemical, or molecular characteristics sampled by the detector. Since a detector should not respond to harmless organisms, it is very difficult to define a harmless simulant with characteristics which will cause the detector to function. A detector with a high false alarm rate is not usable. The burden of unnecessary protective responses and the ensuing loss of confidence in the detector create an untenable situation for the military commander and his personnel.

Chapter 4: Use of Simulants

Introduction

The Committee requested "An evaluation of the utility of simulant versus live-agent testing for carrying out the facility's proposed mission." Chapter 4 provides the evaluation.

As used in this report, the term simulant refers to a surrogate challenge material that has equivalent physical, and/or chemical, and/or biological properties of the agent it mimics; whose properties have been fully documented; and which is essentially harmless. To qualify for selection, simulants must have significantly lower adverse properties (such as pathogenicity and/or toxicity) than the agents they simulate. A simulant can be accepted for use in place of the actual agent only when there is a validated data base that supports accurate extrapolation of the simulant's test results to a battlefield scenario. Doing otherwise would violate scientific standards and procedures. If the simulant has not been validated, then the results must carry a warning that they have no guarantee of reliability.

Advantages of Simulant Use

The Department of Defense endorses the use of simulants because they offer several advantages. They reduce the hazards to people and the environment, though they do not necessarily eliminate the hazards. This in turn reduces safety procedure and monitoring requirements, which saves manpower and equipment expenses. Training is easier and can be more thorough than permitted by actual agents. For example, simulants permit very thorough training in emergency and recovery procedures.

Disadvantages of Simulant Use

The disadvantages of using simulants include the questionable validity of the results and doubts about their applicability. Good simulants are hard to find; there aren't any validated simulants available for any rickettsia, viruses, or toxins, three of the four classes of conventional biological agents.

Before developing and accepting a simulant for a potential biological threat agent the scientist must first know the detailed characteristics of the actual agent. This may require extensive testing of the actual material before simulant development can begin. The inherent difficulty of this task (discussed later) is illustrated by the current lack of available biological agent simulants that are validated for testing.

Experience shows that no single simulant duplicates all the important characteristics of the agent it simulates. This creates problems when the scientist has to show how the simulant testing relates to agent testing. A simulant must be validated for the agent it represents and for the conditions of the test situation. Interpretation of test results must consider any differences. Comprehensive testing usually requires more than one simulant be used, which creates additional problems with simulant and agent correlation. The following sections expand on these considerations.

For situations involving "Life or Death" simulants cannot give the confidence level provided by the real thing. Comprehensive training or evaluation requires using both.

Developing Simulants

The preceding discussion is based principally on traditional, classical biological agents. For the most part this means bacteria, viruses, fungi, and rickettsia. Their basic characteristics are known through open academic and technical sources and from information gained during previous U.S. biological warfare programs. Since safe, closed facilities and procedures to handle these pathogens were available there was little need to investigate simulants for them, especially considering the additional cost and low probability of success.

The application of biotechnology has created an entirely different situation. Living organisms can be altered to increase their toxicity or modify their effects on humans; substances which were too costly to consider can be readily produced in militarily useful quantities; and seemingly innocuous organisms which the body accepts, such as *E. coli* which is normal in human intestines, can be altered to produce deadly substances. Thus the hazard sneaks by the body's normal defenses. The result is a manyfold increase in the number of candidate agents. The technical requirements that protective equipment must satisfy are increased in direct proportion. The potential agents must be analyzed and characterized to develop the details. This itself is a formidable task and requires working with the hazardous materials.

Developing a simulant is an even greater task. First the scientist must identify and select candidate simulants. Then the validation testing requires many experiments to develop the necessary data base. This is multiplied by the number of simulant materials needed to fully represent the principal threat material. Consideration of novel airborne biological organisms further complicates the problem of defining simulants, as does the need to stimulate the effects of new packaging, processing and dissemination technologies on conventional and novel airborne organisms.

In simpler terms, developing simulants requires a great deal of work with toxic materials without any guarantee the simulant development will be successful. Testing with the primary material is often more effective, gives better results, and can be accomplished more expeditiously with less use of pathogenic material.

There is a similar problem with threat evaluation studies, to determine how dangerous a material might be and how it would impact on U.S. operations. Obviously evaluation of potential threat requires use of the threat agent, especially if the sample is obtained through intelligence sources.

Can the Defense Requirements be Met by use of Simulants?

The military requirement for effective biological warfare defense cannot be supported by using only simulants.

— There are no validated simulants for potential threat agents in the following groups: vegetative bacteria, rickettsia, viruses, toxins, fungi, and novel airborne agents.

— Equipment (such as detectors) that depends on biological activity and immunological specificity for action must be tested with biological agents to ensure proper response to the challenge.

— A detector which responds too easily to simulants would not be useful operationally because of its high false alarm rate.

— Characterization of potential threat agents requires use of pathogenic microorganisms and toxins.

— Simulant use is at least a three-variable problem balancing the class of agent against the type of equipment to be challenged against the battlefield scenario to be considered. Then there are further variations and subsets to be considered. Extrapolation of data derived from such a situation is a risky proposition for the decision maker.

There is no reasonable prospect that a total set of simulants could be searched, identified, selected, and validated in time to meet current defense requirements. The Department would make greater use of simulants, where appropriate, if they were available.

Summary

To conclude then, the Department of Defense faces a high technology threat which can present many challenges and variations in a short time. The defensive response must be completed quickly to avoid critical vulnerabilities. Since there aren't any validated simulants for most classes of threat agents the only feasible alternative is to use pathogenic and toxic materials for defense testing. The only alternative to the BATF [Biological Aerosol Test Facility] is the alternative of providing military personnel with defensive procedures and equipment which we *hope* work—this is not responsible.

Index